TARAWA—
76 HOURS OF SHEER, BLOODY, FOULED-UP HELL

Tough, battle-hardened General Holland M. ("Howlin' Mad") Smith, who had directed the Tarawa operation from afar, arrived to survey the scene of carnage before the smoke had settled.

He said to General Julian Smith, gazing across the dead at the awesome row of bunkers and pillboxes, "How did they do it, Julian—how did these boys ever take this place?"

He turned to go and almost directly in his path, a kind of answer met his gaze. A lone marine lay there, with one arm flung across the top of the sea wall; inches away from his outstretched fingers stood a blue flag—a beach marker, signaling the boatwaves where to land. The Marine had planted it with his life. Holland Smith trudged on past the body, tears running down his seamed cheeks.

"You can't help but win," he said, "when you've got men like that on your side."

LINE OF DEPARTURE: TARAWA

MARTIN RUSS

ZEBRA BOOKS

KENSINGTON PUBLISHING CORP.

to *Marge Nickel*
for inspired intervention

ZEBRA BOOKS

are published by

KENSINGTON PUBLISHING CORP.
21 East 40th Street
New York, N.Y. 10016

Published by arrangement with Doubleday & Company

Library of Congress Catalog Card Number 73-15362

First Printing: May, 1978

Printed in the United States of America

CONTENTS

Part IV THE VICTORY

Part I:

PREPARATION

"No bastard ever won a war by dying for his country. He won it by making the other poor bastard die for his country."

—General George S. Patton

1

GENESIS
OF *GALVANIC*

The Gilbert Islands had been a British possession until that day in mid-December 1941 when a Japanese landing party brought it forcibly under the Emperor's "eight-cornered roof."

Several frightened natives watched from the palm tree grove as a sun-helmeted officer, followed by a sword bearer, waded ashore on Betio[1] Island and proclaimed Tarawa Atoll and its white coral sands part of the Greater East Asia Co-prosperity Sphere. Within the hour Japanese soldiers in green uniforms were swarming through the colonial headquarters, seizing furniture, silverware, phonograph records and anything else they could carry—one soldier snatched the British administrator's watch right off his wrist. Before nightfall most of the troops were back aboard the ships, with only a token force left ashore. (The British official was allowed to hail the first inter-island scow that put into the lagoon and turned up in New Zealand a few weeks later, none the worse for wear and lucky to be alive.)

A second token force was dropped at Makin, another atoll in the Gilberts archipelago. The men of these two garrisons, only a hundred and twenty miles apart, spun out their days

---

[1] Pronounced *Bay-sho.*

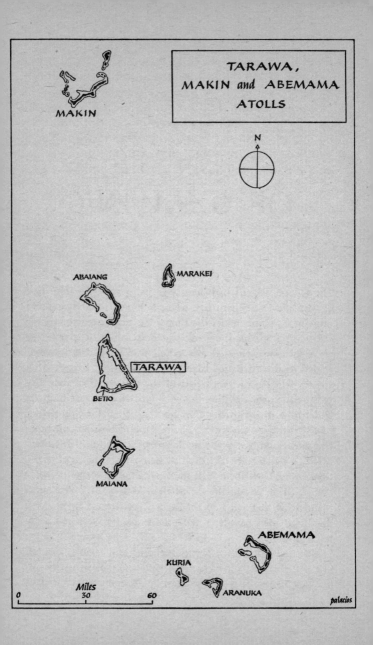

uneventfully until August 1942, when their idyll was rudely shattered by the 2nd Marine Raider Battalion ("Carlson's Raiders"), who staged a sensational hit-and-run attack on Makin, destroying the just-completed seaplane facilities and annihilating the garrison of seventy.[2]

Although the strategists in Tokyo dismissed the raid as a puny attempt to pin down their forces in the Central Pacific while the Americans invaded the Solomons, the revelation of the Gilberts' vulnerability was something of a shock. It was now plain that, unless these outlying islands were fortified and garrisoned in strength, they might easily fall into American hands and serve as bases for a thrust into the Marshalls. Shortly after the Marine raiders' departure, imperial headquarters dispatched a much larger contingent of troops, along with a construction battalion; they arrived at Tarawa and Makin atolls in mid-September. A detachment was shipped on to tiny Abemama, another of the Gilbert Islands seventy-five miles to the southeast.[3] This speck of coral (once dear to the heart of Robert Louis Stevenson) thus became in 1943 the farthest-flung outpost of the Japanese Empire—and possibly the smallest, with a garrison of only twenty-five.

It had already been decided in Tokyo that Betio, the westernmost island of Tarawa Atoll (and the former site of the British headquarters), was to be the keystone of the Gilberts defense system. Under the direction of Rear Admiral Tomanari Saichiro, a superb engineer, it was now converted into nothing less than the most formidable fortress, acre for acre, in the world.

"No military historian who viewed [Betio's] defenses," wrote Samuel Eliot Morison later, "could recall an instance of a small island's having been so well prepared for an attack. Corregidor was an open town by comparison." Saichiro's island fortress was studded with blockhouses and pillboxes, some

[2] "All men are dying serenely in battle," radioed the garrison commander in his final message.
[3] See map, p. 4.

rearing up as high as seventeen feet above the sand, many with interlocking fields of fire. The strength of the blockhouses was impressive by any standard: five-foot-thick concrete walls, superimposed with coconut palm logs of extraordinary resilience, reinforced with angle irons and railroad ties. Several feet of coral detritus and sand had been poured on top; from a distance the blockhouses resembled giant anthills. The pillboxes were smaller versions, half buried, looking something like upside-down grapefruit halves. Between the blockhouses and pillboxes were networks of trenches with compartmented fighting niches; a grenade or shell had to burst in the exact compartment in order to kill its defender. Foxholes were dug on a spider-leg pattern: four or five slit trenches fanning outward from a larger feeder trench. (With a man in each, it would take four or five grenades to kill them, and, being Japanese, the last man was sure to go down fighting.)

Around the edge of the island was a sea wall made of coconut logs clamped together. The American invader was going to have trouble enough getting across the coral reef that surrounded Betio, but equally hazardous would be the attempt to climb over the sea wall, for an American helmet rearing up above the topmost log would be as helplessly conspicuous as a wasp on a windowpane.

Betio absolutely bristled with weapons. There were twenty coast-defense guns, including four eight-inch Vickers guns believed to have been captured from the British at Singapore. There were ten 75-mm. mountain guns and six 70-mm. cannon, along with nine 37-mm. field pieces. The garrison's nine light tanks each mounted 37-mm. cannon, and the innumerable anti-aircraft guns were dual-purpose, which meant that they could shoot at boats as well as planes. Machine guns and rifles were legion. The Betio commander had at his disposal 1,122 well-trained sailors from the 3rd Special Base Force plus 1,497 more from the Sasebo 7th Special Naval Landing Force. Besides these combat troops there was a large contingent of laborers, mostly Koreans: 1,247 from the 111th Construction

Unit and 970 from the 4th Fleet Construction Department. Some of the construction workers took part in the fight to come, but the Betio commander's effectives probably did not number more than 3,000.

The unusually powerful fortifications and garrisoning of Betio in the Gilberts was not an isolated gesture of defiance, for by now the Japanese high command expected an American thrust in the Central Pacific, especially toward those islands with airfields. If such islands were strongly defended, however, the American fleet might be forced to tarry in the target area long enough for Japanese aircraft and submarines to converge in counterattack. Admiral Mineichi Koga's awesome Combined Fleet would then sortie from Truk in the Carolines and destroy the intruders. Betio's defenders, counting on help from afar, were thus motivated to fight stubbornly until that help arrived.

Admiral Saichiro was relieved in September by a stocky, boyish-looking officer with a chestful of campaign ribbons. Whereas Saichiro had been more engineer than combat leader, Rear Admiral Keiji Shibasaki was strictly tactical—and quite ready to defend Betio to the last man. That was very nearly the way it turned out, too, even though the new commander, after inspecting the fortifications, was heard to boast that a million men could not take Betio if they had a hundred years to try. Out of the 4,836 subjects of the Emperor who were unlucky enough to find themselves on Betio Island on the morning of November 20th, 1943, only seventeen Japanese survived the ferocious affair.

Allied intelligence became aware of Betio's burgeoning fortifications when a United States reconnaissance plane spotted the new 4,000-foot airstrip in the summer of 1943. The United States high command had already suspected that the Gilberts were being turned into the kind of impregnable redoubt that the Marshalls and Carolines were reputed to be. By July 20th the decision had been made by the Joint Chiefs of Staff in Washington to invade, conquer and hold the Gilberts for the purpose of setting up an air base "steppingstone" for the great American counteroffensive against the Japanese Empire.

The strategical situation in the summer of '43 was roughly this. In the North Pacific Theater the Americans had ousted the Japanese from their foothold in the Aleutians; the conquest of the Solomons was almost complete (the 3rd Marine Division's invasion of Bougainville on November 1st would wrap it up); and in the Southwest Pacific, Douglas MacArthur's forces were well into New Guinea and preparing to penetrate the Bismarcks. Yet in a year and a half of warfare the Americans had yet to capture a single point which the enemy had not taken since December 7th, 1941. To American planners the capture of the bases in the Gilberts would mark the beginning of a major effort against Japan—the first strategical thrust aimed directly at the heart of the enemy. The rollback phase had ended; the Gilberts campaign would be the start of an unprecedented parade of victories that was to end at Iwo Jima and Okinawa.

There was considerable controversy after the war about the campaign, some critics arguing that the Americans should have gone right into the Marshalls, by-passing the Gilberts and thus—so the argument went—saving the lives lost in that campaign. Others contended that the lessons learned in the Gilberts testing ground saved lives that would have been sacrificed in subsequent operations. The matter has never been settled once and for all, but it is of some small interest to identify the man whose idea it was in the first place to invade the Gilberts archipelago.

Admiral Chester Nimitz, commander of the Pacific Fleet, had recommended in the spring of '43 to Admiral Ernest King (Chief of Naval Operations) that a general offensive should

begin in the Central Pacific with the capture of the Marshalls.
The Joint Chiefs of Staff accordingly ordered their capture
and Nimitz was directed to draw up a strategical plan for the
operation, with the tactics to be left to the man in charge of
the battle force.

Back at his Makalapa headquarters overlooking Pearl Harbor, Nimitz took up the matter with his chief of staff, Vice
Admiral Raymond A. Spruance. A slender, stiffly formal man,
Spruance (who had commanded the victorious forces at Midway in June of '42) now proposed that the Marshalls be approached from the south—that is, through the Gilberts. The
capture of airfield sites there would bring the Marshalls within
effective range of land-based planes and would enable the
Navy to launch its westward drive from a more stable position. Spruance convinced Admiral Nimitz that it would be
wiser, and safer, to seize a first objective that could more
readily be taken with the available slender resources.

Admiral King approved the idea of going into the Gilberts
first, but complicated matters by ordering the additional capture of Nauru, a phosphate island 380 miles west of Tarawa
in the general direction of Truk. Spruance, wary of Koga's
Combined Fleet (based at Truk), was against this from the
start, and put his planners to work on possible alternate targets to present to King at the showdown conference. In the
meantime the Joint Chiefs issued the formal directive to
Nimitz, dated July 20th, giving him the go-ahead to organize
and train the amphibious forces that were to take the Gilbert
Islands plus the island of Nauru. Nimitz code-named the
project Operation *Galvanic* and turned it over to his chief of
staff.

The first thing Spruance did was to tell the admiral he
wanted Kelly Turner to command the amphibious force and
Holland Smith for the landing troops. It was generally agreed
in military circles that an amphibious landing against strong
opposition was the most difficult of all operations, and Spru-

ance wanted the best leaders available. Turner and Smith were the obvious choices.

* * *

Rear Admiral Richmond Kelly Turner, a hard-drinking and often pugnacious fellow from Oregon, was thought to be a master in the art of amphibious warfare. It was Turner who had led the amphibious force that landed the Marines at Guadalcanal. His Marine Corps counterpart-to-be for *Galvanic*, Major General Holland M. Smith, an Alabaman, had been largely responsible for the amphibious doctrine adopted by American forces up to that time. For the past several months Smith had been in charge of Army and Marine amphibious training on the West Coast; Smith-trained (but not -led) troops had landed on Attu Island in the Aleutians in May, defeating the Japanese who had occupied it nearly a year before. Smith had personally witnessed the fantastic *banzai* from out of a cold fog bank on May 29th in which six hundred of the enemy were killed.

In June of '43, Nimitz summoned Smith to Hawaii, intending to take a close look at this man his chief of staff was so eager to recruit. A grandfatherly figure with a bulbous nose, decidedly older-looking than most general officers, Holland M. Smith seemed almost benign behind his round bifocals—until such time as he got the notion that his Marines were somehow being short-changed. Then he would leave no doubt as to why his troops called him "Howlin' Mad" Smith.

Nimitz took Smith along on a sweeping inspection tour, and although the Marine general was satisfied with the condition of the troops he had trained in California, he grew personally more and more depressed at the training-command future he saw stretching out before him. One morning halfway through the tour, as he sat gazing through the window of the Coronado, Nimitz—who had been thumbing through a magazine—abruptly called him to his end of the plane's cabin.

"Holland," he said, "I've decided to bring you out to the Pacific this fall. You'll be in command of all the Marines in the Central Pacific. I think you'll find the job very interesting."

Interesting it would certainly be; but Smith would also find Operation *Galvanic* the most frustrating period in his long career.

2

K ROOM

Holland Smith reported for his new assignment on September 5th, arriving by Pan Am Clipper from San Francisco. Kelly Turner met him at the airport and drove him the twelve miles to Makalapa—where more Navy brass was quartered than anywhere in the world. Ordinarily the admirals and captains lived in houses atop the breeze-swept hill; junior lieutenants occupied more modest quarters at the bottom. Before he knew what was happening, Smith found himself being ushered into lieutenant's quarters. It took a few minutes to sink in, but when it did there was hell to pay. Smith, aroused, was—according to more than one observer—"all mouth." That afternoon his righteous indignation was audible all over Makalapa, and it was not long before he got himself installed in quarters befitting, across the street from Nimitz himself. By way of apology, he was assured that a billeting officer had merely made a stupid blunder.

That settled, Smith, Turner, and Spruance got down to work on *Galvanic*. The Nauru landing was still on; Spruance's staff had not been able to find a suitable alternate target. Smith, glancing through a stack of reconnaissance photos, saw that Nauru was basically a monolith with a hundred-foot cliff rising behind narrow beaches, and concluded on the spot that it would require at least a division to take it. Knowing that the fleet lacked the transports to do the job (what with Tarawa to conquer in the same operation), Smith set to work on a memorandum in which he urged the substitution of Makin Atoll for Nauru Island.

When Admiral King arrived from Washington on the 24th the Nauru question was still up in the air. At a conference attended by King, Nimitz, Spruance, Turner and Smith, the Marine general took out his memo and passed it around. Turner had already read and endorsed it. No one made any comment as the paper went from hand to hand. After King had read it he turned to Raymond Spruance.

"But what would you substitute for Nauru?"

"I agree with Holland. Makin."

King said nothing further on the matter, but on the 27th word came in from the Joint Chiefs: Nauru was out, Makin was in.

And so the plan was finally set. It was to be Tarawa and Makin atolls—plus one minor side show, Abemama. Smith had already assigned the Tarawa target to Major General Julian Smith's 2nd Marine Division, a unit that had a year before helped the 1st Marine Division wrest Guadalcanal and Tulagi from the enemy. Makin Atoll was to be captured by a reinforced regiment of the U. S. Army's 27th Infantry Division. Tiny Abemama would be scouted by a small Marine landing party, whose job it would be to determine whether an amphibious landing in force was necessary.

Like H. M. Smith, bespectacled Julian C. Smith was no one's idea of the typical Marine general. Shy and self-effacing, he spoke with a soft voice and had a slightly dreamy look about him. Smith had not seen action on Guadalcanal, having taken over the 2nd Marine Division after its work there was done; but during his long career (he had been a Marine officer since 1909) he had fought in places like Vera Cruz, Haiti, Santo Domingo and Nicaragua. Smith and his newly acquired division were presently headquartered in Wellington, New Zealand. The fifty-eight-year-old Marine had met Spruance for the first time in August, when the dour admiral came all the way from Hawaii to tell him personally that it was his division that would be attacking Tarawa in late November.

In K Room on the third floor of the Windsor Hotel, overlooking Lambton Harbor, Spruance had spread out a chart of the atoll and the two had pored over it, with members of Smith's staff looking on.

"Looks to me like the reef is going to be our biggest problem," said the general after a few minutes.

Major David M. Shoup, Smith's operations officer—destined to become one of the heroes of Tarawa—made a suggestion at this point. He recalled the tracked amphibious supply-carrying vehicles he had seen on the beach at Guadalcanal; they were called LVTs (landing vehicle, tracked) or "amtracs."

"Seems to me they'd be mighty handy for getting troops across a reef like that one," he commented.

Spruance shook his head. "The landing will have to be made in ship's boats."

It seemed to Shoup that the tracked amphibians were the common-sense solution to the problem of transporting several hundred men across a fringing reef; but the admiral did not elaborate, and it was obvious to Shoup that the subject was closed, at least for then.

Spruance flew out of Wellington the following morning, leaving Julian Smith and his staff to work out a detailed invasion plan. A guard was posted in the corridor outside K Room, which now became the "war room," and Smith began ironing out the thousand and one details of a divisional amphibious landing. Aerial photographs, reconnaissance reports, hydrographic charts—all stamped SECRET—began piling up on the staff officers' desks. It wasn't long before the men who worked in K Room could justifiably call themselves the world's foremost authorities on Betio Island, Tarawa Atoll.

Straddling the Equator just west of the International Date Line, Tarawa lies some twenty-five hundred miles southwest of Pearl Harbor. That particular region of the Pacific was—

and is to this day—very much off the normal shipping lanes; little was known about the place in 1943, because few outsiders had ever been there. From the window of a plane flying high above it, the atoll might be said to look something like a broken-apart white necklace floating on the water.[1] Betio, the principal island, anchors the southwest corner of the roughly triangular atoll and is only 291 acres in area—less than half the size of New York's Central Park. No spot on the island is as much as three hundred yards from the beaches that surround it. In that confined space, on a featureless plain of coral sand and airstrip concrete, six thousand men were soon to die in the Pacific War's bluntest, unsubtlest battle.

[1] An atoll is a natural formation that develops when coral gathers around the base of a mountain that subsequently sinks into the sea. It is the remaining coral collar, built up over aeons, that forms the reef on which sand accumulates to create islands.

3

OONUKI

Like so many young men of his day, Petty Officer Tadao Oonuki, Japanese Imperial Navy, wanted to see something of the war at first hand. Since the fighting began, the only job he had had was driving a truck on routine errands—while many of his boyhood friends from Kasumigaura were meeting the enemy face to face, attaining for themselves a kind of Confucian glory impossible for a truck driver. Although Oonuki had served in several campaign theaters, including China and Indochina, he had yet to hear a single shot fired with intent to kill.

All this was hard on him. In March 1943 he went home on leave and was reassigned to the giant Yokosuka Naval Base; there his embarrassment was aggravated by blood-stirring tales told by the sailors off the warships. To make matters even worse, Oonuki's parents began pressuring him to get married; he had to undergo an agonizingly formal meeting with a young woman they had picked out for him.

One day a call for volunteers appeared on the headquarters bulletin board. Men were needed for "hazardous duty in the south." Oonuki, rejoicing in the opportunity to escape his boring driving duties, signed his name at the bottom. By this simple act he was to join that special fraternity of men the world over who have fought in blood-spilling combat for their country.

* * *

Twelve days later Oonuki and nine other volunteers arrived at Makin Atoll in the Gilberts aboard a cruiser, where they were transferred to a smaller ship and taken to Tarawa. They arrived at the headquarters base on Betio on July 10th and were immediately assigned to the Special Landing Force that made up the nucleus of the Tarawa Atoll garrison. Oonuki was given a new kind of job: instead of a truck, he would now be driving a Type 97 tank that was armed with a 37-mm. cannon plus two 7.7-mm. machine guns. In the event of an enemy attack, he was to help protect the centrally located command post of Rear Admiral Shibasaki.

Oonuki was happy in his new assignment, even though the Gilberts were on an obscure fringe of the war zone. As far as he could foresee, he would put in his time for seven months or so and then return to Japan with his head high. He had volunteered for hazardous duty; it was not his fault that the enemy ignored this particular sector. Quickly he settled into the routine of the place. Life on Betio was good in those days; there was plenty of free time for swimming and fishing. The setting was beautiful—white beaches enclosing a chain of low-lying islands with coconut palms, breadfruit trees, mangroves and sand brush, and a lagoon in the center of it all whose pellucid waters shifted from turquoise to emerald, from cobalt blue to milky green. At night the blues softened to delicate purples, the greens to gentle grays. When the moon rose the place was like something out of a dream.

Oonuki usually spent his evenings drinking sake with his friend, Torpedo Officer Yoshio Tanikaze. The sake ration was not generous, but a man could augment it by swapping food and cigarettes with the garrison's teetotalers. Oonuki and Tanikaze often listened to the news from Tokyo. It was almost always good news; Japan was winning the war in a big way, it seemed. Those who understood English listened occasionally to broadcasts from San Francisco. It was common knowledge that the Americans claimed to have won the battle for the Solomons. Oonuki and most of the others assumed that the high command had merely decided that Guadalcanal was not worth the price and, as they had so wisely done in the Aleutians, ordered the troops withdrawn.

Then came the garrison's first contact with the enemy. It was not very intimidating. Formations of American B-24s were now flying over Betio once a month, coming in from the south to drop their bombs from a high altitude. During the first two raids the bombs were dropped from so high up, in fact, that they missed the target altogether. To Tadao Oonuki and his comrades this was hilarious.

Oonuki was to recall in later years that the Betio garrison began losing its "fighting spirit" at about the time the harmless once-a-month bombings became routine. Life was too easy now. The American air force had proven themselves ineffectual, and as a result the garrison's taut combat readiness slipped away.

On September 18th, however, something happened to snap that martial spirit back to a high degree of tension. That morning Oonuki's friend Tanikaze was out with his torpedo-boat crew on a routine lagoon patrol, when a formation of U. S. Navy carrier planes came swooping in from the east to bomb and strafe the island. Tanikaze turned his boat toward the nearest shore line, Eita Islet, the third island down the chain from Betio. A lone Grumman Hellcat came boring in, spraying a long burst of fifty-caliber bullets alongside the craft and on beyond. The plane banked into the sun and came in for a second pass; Tanikaze was killed a few moments later as he tried to swim to safety. The torpedo boat, filled with holes, sank quickly.

Oonuki sat out the raid huddled inside his Type 97 tank. It would have been easy to run into the admiral's command post, but when he thought of the smell caused by several hundred close-packed sweating bodies in the shelter (something he had endured in drills) he decided to scramble down

the tank hatch instead. He regretted this moment of fastid-
iousness when bullets began churning up the sand all around
him. None hit the tank, but when it was over and the planes
disappeared over the horizon, Oonuki believed he had ex-
perienced enough warfare to last him a lifetime. It was only
the beginning.

That night he took part in the customary evening ceremony, with the men of the garrison turning their faces toward
the faraway palace of the God-Emperor and reciting the
words of the beneficent Imperial Rescript, which showed the
warrior his daily way and reminded him of his sacred mission
and glorious reward, *jimbo,* death in battle. Few of the sailors
expected to find it on Betio. Almost all of them would.

An American civilian correspondent who had accompanied
the raiding planes overoptimistically reported, "Little Tarawa,
heart of the Japanese hornet's nest in the Gilbert Islands, was
smouldering in ruins tonight." A few fighter planes and bombers had been destroyed on the airstrip and twenty men, including Yoshio Tanikaze, had been killed; but Betio was
hardly a ruin. Nor was the garrison at all cowed. The air attack had, in fact, a backlash effect on their morale; from that
day on, the construction battalions drove themselves to great
feats of labor, and the fortifications became all the more impressive. Such was the pulverizing devastation of the battle
for Betio, November 20-23, that few records survived; those
that did reveal a tremendous inflow of cement and building
materials in October and the first two weeks of November.

From the viewpoint of the officers in the Windsor Hotel's K
Room the raid was successful if only because of the excellent
oblique photos snapped by lagoon-skimming camera planes.[1]
Five days after the raid another series of reconnaissance
photos were taken through the periscope of the submarine
Nautilus (the same that had carried Carlson's Raiders to
Makin and back). There was some trouble getting the shots;
Nautilus' periscope had been fitted with a camera bracket,

[1] See photographs 1 and 2.

but three Navy-issue cameras in a row proved faulty. Fortunately for the mission, the executive officer, Lieutenant Commander R. B. Lynch, was an ardent amateur photographer and saved the day with his own Leica. *Nautilus* arrived off Tarawa Atoll on September 23rd and spent several days making a thorough recon of the coral chain, as well as the other two targets of Operation *Galvanic,* Makin and Abemama. The periscope was rotated at each exposure over a long roll of film, recording an almost continuous panorama of beaches.

4

PROBLEM
The Reef

By the end of September Julian C. Smith had assembled a
group of British and New Zealand civilians to help him re-
solve the nagging confusion over the unusual Tarawa tides.
Most of the men of Smith's "foreign legion," as he called
them, had lived in the Gilberts before the war, operating
small steamers or schooners in those waters. One was the
former director of education on Tarawa, Frank L. G. Holland,
who had lived on Betio itself near the Burns-Philp South Sea
Trading Company wharf. Holland had a clear memory of the
sea conditions and warned the Marine general of the irregular
"dodging" tides that sometimes occurred during the neap tide
phase. The other civilians discounted the white-haired Britisher's misgivings, and assured Smith that there would be a
good five feet of water over the reef,[1] more than enough to
float the small Higgins boats all the way in to the beach.

Smith asked the U. S. Coast and Geodetic Survey in Washington to recheck the tide tables he was working with. The
figures were confirmed, and he was back where he started.
Without the amphibious tractors Major David Shoup had

---

[1] The use of the term "reef" here, and throughout, does not refer to
rocky shoals but to a coral shelf sloping gently from the beach to deep
water.

suggested, the troops in their little boats were likely to find themselves scraping bottom several hundred yards out. This meant that the troops might have to wade ashore in slow motion, fearfully vulnerable to enemy fire. Amtracs, made of steel, afforded some measure of protection from that fire and were capable of carrying troops all the way in to the log barrier that rose up a few yards inshore.

"There's no question about it," Smith told his chief of operations. "We've got to talk somebody out of those amtracs."

In early October Julian Smith flew to Hawaii to present his proposed scheme of maneuver and discuss the tide problem with General Holland Smith.

Betio, a flat expanse of coral taken up largely by an airfield, was so small that there was little opportunity for maneuver in the classical sense. Smith's primary tactical problem revolved around where to put his Marines ashore; after that it would be only a matter of short blunt attacks straight ahead. On the south or ocean side of Betio the reef lay five hundred yards out—closer to shore than on the lagoon side; but the constantly washing surf with the whole sweep of the Pacific behind it was a factor that could complicate any landing there. More than that, it was evident from the aerial photos that the enemy commander expected the Americans to approach from that direction—his fortifications were heavier there.

Julian Smith told H. M. Smith that he had decided to send his Higgins boats into the placid Tarawa lagoon and land the assault battalions on the northern shore. (He and Shoup were still in the process of working out the exact boundaries and limits of the three contiguous landing beaches.) He then began to review the reef-and-tide problem which he and his staff had been struggling with, and the danger that with a low-dodging tide a large part of his landing force might become stranded in the lagoon and be cut down as they tried to wade ashore.

"You can see I need amtracs," said the mild-mannered general.

Smith's eyes grew large behind his round bifocals. "I thought you had them."

"I have seventy-five at Wellington. That's enough to get two or three waves ashore. I'll need at least a hundred more."

Smith nodded grimly. "All right, I'll get them for you."

He spoke to Kelly Turner about it that afternoon. The irascible admiral shook his head. "You can count on getting a high-dodger on D-day," he said. "You won't need amtracs."

Smith tried to stay calm. "Kelly, it's like this—I've got to have those amtracs. We could take a hell of a licking without them."

They began to argue, and Smith finally burst out: "No amtracs, no operation!"

Turner was not often given ultimatums, but he finally agreed to assign a hundred more amphibian tractors to the 2nd Marine Division. They were to be brought in from the naval base at Samoa—although Turner warned that he was not sure he could get them transferred in time for the operation. No one ever found out exactly why Turner and Spruance were reluctant to supply the landing force with the equipment it so obviously needed, and Holland Smith went to his grave convinced that it was just another example of the Navy's callous indifference to the Marines. Whatever the reason, it exemplified the lack of foresight that was evident throughout this poorly planned and badly bungled operation.

Julian Smith was relieved to hear about the additional amtracs, but that was the only good news he was to hear in Hawaii; his other proposals were turned down flat. He had asked for a tactical feint against the ocean side or south shore, to draw enemy troops away from the actual landing beaches. This was brushed aside; Turner explained, reasonably enough, that he could not set up another transport area without taking away half the invasion force's destroyer support. Smith had also asked for a preliminary landing on the neighboring island of Bairiki, so that artillery could be set up to blast enemy positions on Betio. Holland Smith turned that one down, explaining that there was too little time to arrange for that kind of extra support. With a chart and a pair of dividers he showed J. C. Smith that such a preliminary landing would give the Japanese time to stage their reserve troops through Nauru and the Marshalls. Speed of conquest was essential. Betio must be quickly overrun, its airfield cleared and made ready for American planes, and the thin-skinned transports and supply ships withdrawn from the dangerous waters as soon as practicable.

"No time for anything fancy," said the elder general.

Julian Smith surprised everyone by asking to be formally absolved of the decision to seize Betio before any of the other atoll islands. For a moment there was a stunned silence around the conference table; it was an unusual request, to say the least. Smith repeated it; he wanted everything spelled out on paper. Holland Smith impatiently snapped a command over his shoulder and a staff assistant went to work at a desk in the anteroom. Julian Smith was satisfied; the landing plan was cut and dried, allowing him no leeway at all.

There was one more bit of bad news. H. M. Smith told him that one of the division's three infantry regiments was to be held in reserve in the waters off Makin. Julian Smith was being asked to swallow the idea of capturing Betio with the Second Marines and the Eighth Marines, while the Sixth Marines were being retained as a floating reserve a hundred and twenty miles away.[2] Turner had decided that the Army troops on Makin would probably need help sooner than the Marines on Betio. It was a remarkably poor decision, since the Makin garrison was small and the fortifications insignificant compared with what the Second and Eighth Marines were going to face to the south.

[2] The Second, Sixth, and Eighth Marines were the three infantry regiments of the Second Marine Division.

Thus Major General Julian Smith was confronted with the dismal prospect of trying to secure a foothold on a strongly held island with an initial force of only 1,464 men—assuming that all of them made it ashore, which would certainly not be the case. Waiting to drive the invaders back into the sea was a garrison of some 2,700 heavily armed sailors, plus labor and support troops numbering around 2,200. Once the Marines carved out a solid beachhead, the rest of the division could be poured ashore and a numerical advantage built up. The opening phase of the battle, however, determining the size and character of that beachhead, would be a toe-to-toe affair with the defenders holding the edge in numbers.

Major Henry Drewes (Jersey City, N.J.), the commander of the division's amphibian tractor battalion, had only just said farewell to his nineteen-year-old son when General Smith returned from the disheartening conference in Hawaii. Corporal Richard Drewes, a veteran of Guadalcanal, had contracted malaria and was being sent to the States. He had been allowed to stop off at Wellington briefly, and his proud father showed him the sights of the harbor city before putting him on the plane to Honolulu. (It was to be their last meeting.) Soon after his son's departure, Drewes was called into K Room and told that, in the upcoming operation, he had better expect the worst since his amphibian tractors would be the initial targets of enemy fire. Smith then made an ominous suggestion: he told Drewes that he would be wise to get more armor plating on his amtracs.

Drewes searched around the city and suburbs until he found a pile of 9-mm. steel that was gathering rust outside a factory northwest of town. He bought the steel and set about designing armor plating to fit the front of the tracked vehicles that would carry the first three waves in to Betio. The steel was cut and shaped at the General Motors plant in Wellington. Drewes's second in command, Captain Henry

Lawrence, later said that he was certain the armor saved many lives.[3] Its greatest value—as far as the success of the battle was concerned—was as a morale booster for the amtrac crews, especially the machine gunners who rode up forward, partially exposed to the enemy. There was no question that, with a bit of armor to stand behind, a man's fighting spirit was likely to take on a more aggressive character. At Betio the fighting spirit of the individual Marine was to be more severely tested than in any other Pacific battle.

[3] After the battle the surviving amtrac crew members were inclined to disagree; there were only a relative handful of them left.

5

CORRESPONDENT SHERROD

Three thousand miles north of Honolulu, on the fog-shrouded Aleutian island of Attu, a memorial service was being held for the U. S. Army soldiers who had died in its recapture. *Time-Life* correspondent Robert Sherrod, a sensitive, eagle-beaked man in his thirties, stood among the troops listening to the chaplain's eulogy. Earlier that day he had hiked across the plateau between Holtz Bay and Massacre Bay, counting the Japanese corpses that lay sprawled there. One of the Army intelligence officers had shown him a diary taken from one of the bodies, pointing with a callous chuckle at the line:

> *I will gladly die today, for it is the anniversary of my father's death.*

Sherrod had been in the Aleutians for three weeks and was fed up with the clammy fogs and carrion-smelling silences, and the boredom. When a high-ranking officer told him, off the record, that the next big American offensive would probably take place in the Central Pacific, Sherrod felt a sudden surge of excitement. This was something he wanted to be in on—the opening curtain for a new theater of operations. It would not be cold and foggy or boring in the Central Pacific, of that he was certain. The U. S. Navy would have all the room it needed in a sun-drenched sea to maneuver; that might be a fabulous thing to see.

He wangled a berth aboard the next ship sailing for Hawaii. Day by day the skies grew clearer, the water bluer, the air warmer as they entered the balmy zones. From Hawaii he made his way to the mainland and across the continent to see his editors in Rockefeller Center. It did not take long to sell them on his idea, and for the next few days he shuttled back and forth on crowded trains between New York and Washington, tying up loose ends and saying good-by to his family. At last he was off, arriving in San Francisco barely in time to catch the evening seaplane for Honolulu—actually running up to its side door as it rolled down the ramp.

Three days later he was sitting in the rear seat of a Douglas dive bomber that was taking part in a raid on the already legendary Wake Island—an isolated patch of sand 2,000 miles west of Hawaii where, in December 1941, a handful of U. S. Marines had held out for days while looking over their shoulders for reinforcements that never came. The air strike was a dazzling experience for the civilian Sherrod, and when the planes turned back to the carriers it almost seemed to him as if Wake might dissolve into the sea, such was the volume of fiery smoke arising from it.

This strike, carried out in early October of '43, had an important bearing on the upcoming Operation *Galvanic*. It convinced Tokyo that the American fleet was preparing to attack and invade Wake, rather than the Gilberts or Marshalls. That conviction was strengthened when on October 17th a daring Japanese pilot flew directly over Pearl Harbor (the first to do so since the attack on December 7th, 1941), saw how few ships were in berth, and escaped to the northwest before pursuit planes could get off the ground. Where were all the ships? Headquarters Tokyo believed that the United States fleet was lurking somewhere a few hundred miles off Wake, awaiting favorable weather conditions before launching a landing force.

When Sherrod arrived back in Hawaii, for the third time in as many weeks, he learned he had been assigned to the Makin phase of *Galvanic*. This was a disappointment; he had wanted to see the Marines in action, not the GIs again. He decided to try and get the assignment changed. As a civilian who did not have to pay strict attention to "proper channels," he appealed directly to Admiral Turner and was switched without fuss to the Tarawa phase of the operation.

Robert Sherrod was to make many landings with the Marines before V-J Day; only one, the first, fascinated him to the extent that he wrote a book about it.[1]

[1] See Bibliography.

6

GOOD-BY
TO WELLINGTON

Although the identity of the upcoming target remained a secret among a handful of officers, the Marines on North Island could not help guessing that an operation of some sort was imminent—the harbor was filling up with troopships.

New Zealand suddenly became very dear to the Marines. Of all the distant duty stations and liberty towns of World War II, none matched Wellington, New Zealand, for its friendliness to foreign troops. Thousands of young men from the 1st and 2nd Marine Divisions had been invited to Wellington homes, where they were treated with unfailing hospitality, respect and affection. Often the host and hostess had sons fighting in Anzac units in North Africa and elsewhere, and some had lost sons in battle. Moreover the American Marines were looked on as "protectors of the Dominion"; their stand in the Solomons had blunted the Japanese advance that had threatened the Antipodes. Whatever the reasons, the people of Wellington felt drawn toward the lonesome, boisterous young men so far from home who would only too soon now be facing the enemy again.

Now they swarmed to their last liberties ashore, filling the tea parlors and movie houses and grog shops. There was dancing at the Hotel Cecil—or if a fellow had a little extra jack he took his date to the Grand or even the St. George. For special occasions such as wedding parties (and more than five hundred Marines married local girls) it had to be the Majestic Cabaret.

During the final week of October, the Marines began boarding ship. The official word was that the division was going to stage a full-scale practice landing at Hawkes Bay, a few miles up the coast, and then return to Wellington. Julian Smith solemnly briefed officers of the New Zealand Air Force on their part in providing mock supporting air strikes for the exercise. He even made arrangements with the railway to transport the division's heavy equipment back to the city. It was all an elaborate hoax. Smith had never forgotten how the 1st Marine Division sailed from Wellington fifteen months earlier with the newspapers full of the impending attack on Tulagi. He was determined to get his troops out of town under the "Hawkes Bay maneuvers" smoke screen.

Finally, on the afternoon of October 31st, with every man and every piece of equipment on board the ships, Smith and Major Shoup—literally the last two Marines ashore—hailed a cab and told the driver to take them to Government House. A few minutes later they were sitting in the office of Sir Cyril Newall, the Governor General of New Zealand. They told him that the 2nd Marine Division would not be back.

"You're the only one in New Zealand who knows it," said Smith.

It was a strangely poignant moment, and the three men stood silently. Then Sir Cyril took the general's hand and told him that the people of his country would be sorry indeed to hear that the American Marines had gone. He wished him luck with his venture, "wherever it takes you and your splendid lads."

Smith and Shoup returned to the dock to see hundreds of melancholy Marines standing along the railings, watching the sun set over the hills of the city.

By morning, November 1st, 1943, the ships were moving

out to sea. Behind them, in the lovely city of Wellington, hotel closets stood full of Marine clothing, Marine-registered cars were parked in the streets, and out in the countryside countless young women looked forward to weekend dates, not knowing they would be stood up.

7

SHOUP'S NEW ASSIGNMENT

The convoy was designated Southern Attack Force, and made up roughly half the total strength of *Galvanic*. The other half, Northern Attack Force, carrying the Army's 165th Regimental Combat Team (of the 27th Infantry Division), was about to set sail from Hawaii. Formerly part of the New York National Guard, the 27th was commanded by still another Smith: Major General Ralph C. Smith, United States Army. Smith had studied, and later lectured, at France's École de Guerre and was highly regarded in Army circles as a tactician. His troops had not yet been tested in combat. Marine General Holland Smith, his immediate superior, already harbored some misgivings about the unit and its leadership; the troops had seemed slipshod and careless during the maneuvers he observed in Hawaii, and Ralph Smith himself appeared to lack the fire and drive which in a Marine officer was considered basic.

Holland Smith had a more pressing problem at the moment. He was, once again, embroiled. In Nimitz's written order outlining the tasks of those who would share the leadership of *Galvanic*, Smith was unable to find his own name. He raced through the paragraphs again. Sure enough, his name was missing. Evidently the Navy planned to employ the Fifth Amphibious Corps while its commander twiddled his thumbs back at Pearl Harbor. The insult was, to Smith's mind, blunt and unequivocal; he stormed over to Spruance's office, vibrating with righteous indignation.

"Who is responsible for this?" he wanted to know. He suspected it was Lieutenant General Robert Richardson, the overall Army commander in the Central Pacific, a man Smith believed was intent on grabbing all the glory for the Army in the defeat of Japan, and only too ready to discredit Marine leadership. Unflappable Raymond Spruance calmly apologized for the mix-up and assured Smith he was needed on the operation. Smith did not press the matter further and everything seemed all right again—until he learned that Richmond Kelly Turner was to remain in command of the amphibious operation from start to finish. This was a blow indeed; Smith had expected to assume command ashore once his troops had established a beachhead. His blood up again, he stalked over to Turner's office and a long argument began. A member of Spruance's staff refereed the argument for over an hour, finally asking the admiral to intervene and lay down a dictum.

Spruance shook his head. "I've chosen those two because they're intelligent and reasonable. Let them work it out."

Smith lost the argument in the end, and it was a bitter loss. He was to sail with the assault force flagship and was officially in command of the landing forces, but no tactical order of his was to take effect without Turner's approval. Turner's operations plan was vague concerning the general's duties; he was to "advise the Assault Force Commander on the employment of the landing force and the use of reserves." As it turned out, Smith made only one decision relating to Tarawa, and of course he had to get Turner's approval first. The fact of the matter is, he was very nearly superfluous.

By now every Marine in the convoy knew that the "Hawkes Bay maneuvers" was a cover-up for something bigger. On the night of November 6th the old salts among them smelled land, and at dawn the next day a plateau-topped island stretched long arms on either side of the ships that were now dropping anchor in Mele Bay off the island of Efate, New Hebrides, four hundred miles north of New Zealand. The Marines could see coconut groves and cane fields, and in the distance the town of Vila with the governor's mansion on the hill.

During that week the Marines made two practice landings, both of which proceeded satisfactorily. Many of the Navy officers were by this time almost smugly confident. Little Betio was to shudder under the weight of high explosives hurled into it from three battleships, four cruisers and nine destroyers. Never before had such powerful seaborne batteries been massed against such a diminutive target, and not a few Marines expected to ride comfortably ashore and routinely set up their tents while burial teams disposed of the shell-mangled enemy. In an officers' briefing at Efate, Rear Admiral Howard Kingman, commander of the fire-support group, pompously declared:

"Gentlemen, we will not neutralize Betio. We will not destroy it. . . . We will obliterate it!"

Another officer boasted: "We're going to steam-roller that place until hell wouldn't have it."

Julian Smith sobered them with a reminder that the Marines were going to have to go ashore and capture whatever was left and that, unlike the ships, the only armor a Marine could count on was his dungaree jacket.

Captain Herbert Knowles, commander of the transport group, was not impressed by Kingman's grandiose prediction. He had witnessed a similar bombardment of Gavutu Island in the Solomons, just before the landing of a Marine paratroop outfit. From sun-up to noon this little island had been bombed, strafed and shelled, yet the Japanese were able to put up a stiff fight afterward.

Major David Shoup was another skeptic. He had studied the 1915 Gallipoli campaign and remembered that the British thought they had "obliterated" the defenses there, too, until hordes of Turkish infantry rose up out of holes to bloodily repel the landing force.

Colonel William McN. Marshall, commander of the assault regiment, was a believer. During a break in one of the shipboard conferences he sidled up to Shoup in the passageway and asked, in a hushed and worried voice:

"What in hell are we going to do with *five thousand Jap bodies?*"

David Monroe Shoup (Battleground, Ind.) was one of the more interesting characters connected with the Tarawa campaign. A stocky moonfaced fellow with a high, harsh voice and a wary look in his eye, he seemed outwardly to be the kind of blasphemous, coarse-talking extrovert the Corps is known for. But there was another side to him, known to few (for Shoup was something of a loner), exemplified best perhaps by his tenderly guarded collection of sake warming bottles and the occasional poem he wrote. His fellow officers knew him only as a capable officer and something of a wag.

During the K Room stage of preparations Shoup had sparked a good deal of laughter with a certain intelligence coup. The Japanese had solved the sanitation problem on Betio by building latrine stalls out over the water, rickety wooden affairs that were clearly discernible in the aerial photos. By methodically toting up the number of latrines and working out a probable ratio of buttocks to holes, Shoup came up with an estimated count of the number of men in the garrison; and a remarkably good guess it was, as he learned later. Shoup also figured out where "officers' country" was by studying the shrapnel-stopping baffles outside the entrances to the more elaborate shelters. In one particular blockhouse they were positioned so that a vehicle could be driven between them and the entrance; Shoup correctly guessed that this was the island's command post. It was not a brilliant deduction, but he was proud of it anyway.

His principal contribution to the planning phase was the

landing order, which called for 2nd Battalion, Second Marines, and 2nd Battalion, Eighth Marines (2/2 and 2/8), to hit the beach on either side of the 700-yard-long pier that jutted into the lagoon and spanned the entire reef from shore to the deep water drop-off. The remaining assault unit, 3rd Battalion, Second Marines (3/2), would land at the same time on the right of 2/2. All three battalions, abreast, would then strike inland until they reached the opposite shore of the island. It was as simple a plan of assault as any operations officer ever conceived.

There was one serious flaw. Red Beach 1 included the only irregular shore line on Betio, a deep cove indenting the island just east of its northwestern tip. 3/2 was going to have to land in that cove, exposed to enfilade fire from both flanks as well as that from straight ahead. Most armchair strategists would today agree it would have been wiser to put the battalion ashore on the other side of a shortened Red Beach 3. In any case, no one should have been sent into that cove; a large percentage of the Marines who died in the battle did their dying there.

Two days before the Southern Attack Force was scheduled to leave Efate, Colonel Marshall suffered a heart attack while climbing down the debarking nets. It was only a mild attack, yet Julian Smith had no choice but to relieve him of his duties in the forthcoming operation. The general called Major Shoup into his cabin.

"Somebody's got to take over for Marshall," he said. "I'm promoting you to lieutenant colonel."

Shoup was momentarily stunned, but not overawed; he thought that with luck he could handle the new assignment. Except for Smith, there was no one in the division with a more complete grasp of the battle plan than David Shoup. And so it was set; he was to command the three assault battalions (Crowe's 2/8, Amey's 2/2, Schoettel's 3/2) plus one reserve battalion, until such time as the beachhead was well enough established for the general himself to come ashore. Thus the officer who had done much of the tactical planning was now going to command the actual beachhead—an unusual if not quite unique situation.

The matter of the tide came up again at the last minute when Frank Holland, the former director of education on Tarawa, realized to his dismay that the Americans were definitely going to try and cross the reef on the neap tide. The retired British Army officer sought out Julian Smith at once.

"That information I gave your people before," he explained, "was based on a flood tide. I never dreamed you'd try and land on the neap!"

He went on to say that in all his years on Betio he had never seen more than three feet of water over the reef at the neap. The Higgins boats would need *at least* that to float the troops all the way in to the beach.

Smith grimly called another meeting of the captains and pilots who had sailed the Gilberts in prewar years. In spite of Holland's forebodings, the group consensus was still that there would be enough water on D-day to float the landing boats across the reef at neap tide.

Smith was not reassured. In the meantime Admiral Turner's staff had finished their thorough study of the problem and had come up with the conclusion that "during high water neap tides the reef off the north coast of Betio is covered by from one to two feet of water." Their firm prediction that there would *not* be enough water was wasted on Kelly Turner, however, and in settling on November 20th for D-day (an unnecessary rush date that could as easily have been set for five weeks later, when the tide would be more favorable during the early morning hours), several hundred Marines who might otherwise have survived were instead doomed to die.

8

THE CORPS

Fueling was completed and, on November 13th, Admiral Harry Hill's Southern Attack Force sailed through the Bungo Strait into the open Pacific. Of the Marines, no one except Smith and a handful of his officers knew where they were headed. The convoy's zigzag course crossed and then re-crossed the International Date Line; that week had two Sundays and no Thursday at all. One thing was certain—they were heading in a northerly direction, for the color of the sea was deepening to cobalt and the soft cloud masses of the tropics piled up majestically on the horizon.

Seasickness began to be a problem—not a serious one, but something hundreds of Marines had to deal with. Robert Sherrod, aboard the troopship *Zeilin*, heard one green-faced officer groan bravely, "Roll, you son of a bitch—I don't give a damn." Sherrod himself, only slightly affected by the malady that makes strong men yearn for oblivion, spent a lot of time watching the Marines, trying to pin down what it was that made them different. He had been disappointed by the poor quality of the U. S. Army soldiers on Attu; the troops aboard the *Zeilin* were clearly another breed.

Marines had always been considered as shock troops, their traditional mission being to capture beachheads and hold them until garrison forces arrived. Battalion for battalion, the Marines were the most fearsomely efficient troops on either side in World War II—not because they were braver or had God on their side, but because Marine recruits were inspired from the beginning with the conviction that they belonged to a select and elite legion, and because of the tradition of loyalty which meant in practical terms that an individual Marine trusted and relied on his comrades to an extraordinary degree, and that he himself was reliable. Most Marines of that day believed that it was better to die than let one's comrades down in combat. The ultimate pay-off of this esprit de corps was a headlong aggressiveness that won battles. Ernest Hemingway, who knew something of men in war, wrote, "I would rather have a good Marine, even a ruined one, than anything in the world when there are chips down."

It was the boot-camp training these volunteers endured at Parris Island that established the foundation of this proud military attitude. For eight to ten weeks the individual volunteer ("boot") was hermetically sealed in a hostile environment, every moment calculated to prepare him to function smoothly on the edge of an abyss, subject to such harassment and confusion—very much like combat itself—that it spawned in his homesick heart a desperate yearning for order, and finally a love of that order and a clear understanding that in its symmetry lay his safety and survival.

The men aboard the troopships, trained for the abyss, were now heading directly toward it. On Betio there was to be no "rear area," and every man who set foot on that coral dot in the Pacific became as familiar with death as one can be without actually experiencing it.

9

THE FINAL LEG

On November 14th the weather decks of the troopship *Zeilin* were crowded as usual with Marines, some cleaning weapons, some playing cards, some reading or writing letters. Mostly the men sat staring out to sea, alone with their thoughts. Halfway through the afternoon, Admiral Hill ordered the following message wigwagged from ship to ship:

Give all hands general picture of projected operation.

Within ten minutes every man in the convoy knew what the target was. On the troopship *Heywood* four sailors carried a heavy sand table on deck and the Marines immediately swarmed around it, marveling at the model island—the tiny palm trees, the blockhouses and warehouses and gun emplacements. A sign on the side announced:

BETIO

PRINCIPAL ISLAND OF TARAWA ATOLL

The island was oddly shaped. Some thought it resembled a sea horse; others a musket complete with lock, stock and barrel. Most thought it looked like a bird, upside down, with the pier representing the legs.

Sealed packets of maps, photographs and orders were broken open aboard all ships. Clusters of men, intense and attentive in the sweltering equatorial heat, listened as their officers filled them in on what to expect. As Julian Smith had directed, they were told about the reef and warned that they might have to wade across it, unless they were lucky enough to be riding in one of the first three (amtrac-borne) waves.

Late that afternoon, via the talk-between-ships hookup, Smith read his battle message to the division. "I know you will decisively defeat and destroy the treacherous enemies of our country," he said. "Your success will add new laurels to the glorious tradition of our Corps. Good luck and God bless you all."

The mighty task force bored on toward its goal.

Correspondent Sherrod got to know a few of the officers aboard the *Zeilin.* Two in particular impressed him.

Lieutenant William Deane Hawkins (El Paso, Tex.) had a certain cowboy look about him and was handsome despite the burn scars on his face. Everyone called him Hawk. He had made something of a reputation for himself on Guadalcanal, leading long-range reconnaissance patrols that stayed in the jungle for days. For *Galvanic,* he commanded the Scout-Sniper Platoon, a select group of stalwarts who would be the first ashore on D-day. Scheduled to cross the line of departure fifteen minutes ahead of the first wave, they were to land on the end of the long pier and wipe out any machine-gun positions along its seven-hundred-yard length. This was an important task, on which the safety of the landing force depended; any Japanese gunners emplaced in the pier would be able to enfilade the waves in both directions, while in friendly hands it could provide direct communication with the shore.

Sherrod talked with Hawkins and learned something of his background. He had worked as a ranch hand and railroad brakeman before joining the Marines in '41. The scars he had got as a child, running into his mother while she was carrying a pan of hot water. Sherrod picked up a bit more about him after the war, when he got a letter from Hawkins' mother asking for details of her son's death. He learned among other things that Hawkins had left El Paso for the last time with a distinct premonition that he would die in battle. Bidding farewell to his boyhood pal, Ballard McClesky, he had said: "Mac, I'll see you someday—but not on this earth."

Someone said later that William Deane Hawkins was born to be a Marine hero.

The other officer was a Bible-quoting New Englander named Evans Fordyce Carlson—whose Raiders had made the strike on Makin the year before. Colonel Carlson, a lanky Lincoln-looking fellow and something of an oddball as far as the Corps was concerned, had traveled through China in the thirties, marching with Mao Tse-tung's legendary Eighth Route Army, studying the cadre system that is today one of the main tools of discipline and morale in Communist armies around the world. Carlson wrote two books about the Red Chinese Army, and introduced the *gung ho* (work together) concept to the Marines. Corps headquarters was not particularly interested in the cadre system, but Carlson was nevertheless given the opportunity of organizing and training the 2nd Marine Raider Battalion and was allowed to put a few of the "Chicom" methods into practice. Headquarters was impressed with the unit's effectiveness on Makin and Guadalcanal, and the Raiders themselves were impressed by their leader's personal courage.[1] Carlson, looked on from above as someone almost approaching the crackpot level, was never given command of anything larger than a battalion. For Operation *Galvanic* he was assigned the role of observer for the then-forming 4th Marine Division. Although he had no specific duties during the operation, Carlson was to make himself as useful as any man on Betio.

On November 17th the dread of imminent battle dropped over the Marines like a pall, when the loudspeakers announced:

"Now hear this. We are entering enemy waters. You will

[1] Shoup: "He may have been Red but he wasn't yellow."

exercise every precaution to avoid disclosing our position: you will take care to throw nothing over the side. The smoking lamp is out at sunset."

And there was a definite upsurge of religious fervor. Chaplain Wyeth Willard (Scituate, Mass.) began holding baptisms aboard the troopship *Sheridan,* using the rear observation turret, with sea water pumped in, as a baptistry. Willard, an earnest and deliberate fellow of middle age, was the sole chaplain left from the original eight who had made the Guadalcanal landing. His nerves had been stretched to the breaking point in that campaign but now, heading for Tarawa with the Eighth Marines after months of peaceful churchly labors in New Zealand, he felt rested and full of zeal.

The chaplain knew Shoup well; he had played innumerable checker games with him at Paekakariki and won them all, much to the then-major's disgruntlement. He knew William Hawkins too—had slept in the same tent with him in the Solomons and was familiar with his reputation for reckless bravery. Willard was anxious to see a little action himself; it was not enough to comfort the dying and bury the dead. During the first week at sea he had gone to the cabin of Major Lawrence C. Hays, commander of 1st Battalion, Eighth Marines, and told him that he wanted to land with the initial wave.

Hays shook his head. "Colonel Hall would never forgive me if anything happened to you," he said.

Bitterly disappointed, Willard went shambling back to his own cabin. It did not take him long, however, to decide to go over Hays's head and contact Colonel Elmer Hall aboard the *Monrovia,* using the blinker light system. He composed the following message and presented it for relay:

> *Chaplain Willard earnestly requests permission*
> *to land with 1/8.*

The only question was, would Major Hays relay it? The officer read the message and glanced up. Willard's face was tense with silent pleading. Hays chuckled and gave in.

"Okay, Chaplain. You're on."

Willard turned away grinning and elated, convinced that if he shared the dangers and hardships of the men on Betio "they would more readily accept my message of Christ."

* * *

Several times a day the loudspeakers blared, "Protestant services will be held at 1700 on Number 7 hatch," or "Catholic mass is now being held on Number 4 hatch." Willard, a Baptist minister, was kept busy and he sorely missed his former helper, Sergeant William C. Culp (West Palm Beach, Fla.). A tall, dignified, doe-eyed young man, Culp had been in the Corps four years and—as Willard put it—had got in with the wrong crowd and started drinking too much. Willard befriended him, converted him to the Baptist ways, which included abstinence from liquor, and made him his ministerial assistant. Culp served him well for many months, and the middle-aged chaplain grew fond of him.

As the months passed, he began to see that Culp possessed inherent leadership ability and was stagnating in his present job. Somewhat timidly the chaplain consulted Colonel Hall on the matter. He was told that there was a desperate need in the rifle companies for non-commissioned officers.

"If you can do without an assistant," the regimental commander told him, "I can certainly place him."

When Willard mentioned all this to Culp, the sergeant agreed to apply for transfer. His willingness gladdened and relieved the chaplain; he knew that he had put the young man directly on the spot.

When Culp reported to Captain Maxie Williams, his new commanding officer, the welcome was anything but warm.

"I'm sorry to see you come into my company," he was told. "You've been a chaplain's clerk too long. But I'll give you one chance."

Culp said that was all he wanted.

Captain Williams' new squad leader went on to distinguish

himself in the fighting on Guadalcanal and was promoted to platoon sergeant. Soon after that Williams, recognizing Culp's leadership potential as the chaplain had, recommended him for a commission. Sergeant William C. Culp became Lieutenant Culp.

Going into battle as a platoon leader is not quite the same as going into battle as a chaplain's assistant and the young officer must have wondered, as the ship plowed on toward Tarawa, if perhaps it wouldn't have been better if the chaplain had let things lie.

10

THE APPROACH

At D-day-minus-3 Julian Smith got word from Seventh Air Force that three Liberator bombers had flown over Betio at twenty-five hundred feet and that none of the crewmen had spotted any sign of life. They had received "practically no anti-aircraft fire," the report said. There were some who believed that the planes had not been fired on at all. Before the day was over the Liberator story had been passed around the convoy, and many of the men thought that the operation was sure to be "another Kiska." (When U. S. Army troops landed on that Aleutian island the previous August, immediately after the recapture of Attu, they found that the Japanese had slipped away in the fog.) Robert Sherrod heard an artillery officer declare himself ready to bet that the Marines would likewise find Betio Island deserted. "There won't be a damned Jap on Tarawa," predicted the transport surgeon. "And I'll bet we haven't got an alternate target. Why in hell don't we just take this force and keep going to Tokyo?"

Sherrod himself was very close to believing that the enemy had evacuated Tarawa Atoll; but it was more wish than prediction.

The two separate convoys, one from New Zealand and one (the Northern Attack Force) from Hawaii, were now converging on a lonely spot in the Pacific, a rendezvous point with no land in sight. Already preceding the convoys to the target area itself was the submarine *Nautilus,* an old haunter of these waters. The sub had departed Pearl Harbor on November 8th, carrying the scouting party that would land on Abemama. *Nautilus* was to periscope-scout Betio first, however—for the second time that fall.

Early on the morning of the 18th (D-minus-2) the battleship *Colorado*'s observation plane spotted the Northern Attack Force not far to the northwest—the linkup was imminent. That convoy was in turn spotted a little later by a Japanese search plane, which immediately turned tail and disappeared over the western horizon.

Lieutenant Kichi Yoshuyo, the search plane's pilot, had already transmitted the news of his sensational discovery in the *Kana* code (by which the Japanese language can be spelled):

> *Enemy contact report. Fleet sighted. Several carriers and other types too numerous to mention. . . .*

And soon the garrisons on Kwajalein and Nauru and Truk had the news: enemy fleet approaching the Gilberts! On Betio, Admiral Keiji Shibasaki issued orders to "defend to the last man . . . and destroy the enemy at the water's edge."

Next morning, D-minus-1, Hill's radarmen discerned the presence of a Japanese plane some sixty miles west of the Southern Attack Force. It was a four-engined Mavis, and when it was still forty-five miles from the convoy a trio of carrier planes from *Suwanee* sent it down in flames. In one sense, the opening shot had been fired, although it was only an isolated incident that took place hundreds of miles from the target area; but the main show would not begin for twenty-four hours.

At last the two convoys sighted each other's superstructures over the horizon, and soon they were headed in a parallel course straight for the Gilberts. Together they comprised the most powerful force in naval history up to that time.

Before noon a submarine contact was reported to Hill, and he detached two destroyers to investigate. Throughout the afternoon they played a game of cat and mouse with the sub, catching up with the convoy late in the day to report a probable "kill."[1]

Hill's force, covering an eight-mile square of ocean, had been steering northwesterly for a designated point: latitude 1° 6′ N, longitude 174° 50′ E. At 2:51 p.m. that point was passed and the formation swung to a due-west course, beginning the final leg of its voyage to Tarawa. Kelly Turner's Northern Attack Force, however, churned on straight for Makin, a hundred miles farther on, and soon the convoys were once again out of sight of each other.

The destroyers *Ringgold* and *Dashiell*, slated for an early entrance into Tarawa lagoon next morning, transferred their secret codes to the flagship—the battleship *Maryland*. Out ahead of the convoy now, *Ringgold* was on the lookout for deserted Maiana Atoll, the last guiding mark for the force in its approach to the target. Just before sundown a small convoy bringing the hundred additional amtracs from Samoa reported in—welcome news for Admiral Hill and J. C. Smith. This little convoy proceeded to cross the admiral's bow and take station to starboard. Hill reduced the speed of the entire force to ten knots, for wind and current were shoving the ships along too quickly. (Hill's careful approach was almost ruined by inaccurate charts. It turned out that Betio had been oriented incorrectly on the Admiralty charts he was using, with the island's long tail pointing 139° instead of 128°. Fortunately the submarine *Nautilus* discovered and reported the error in time to prevent the convoy's sailing past Tarawa and losing a lot of time in a second approach.)

Nautilus was having her worst day of the war. Commander W. D. Irvin had spent a good deal of time at Pearl Harbor testing various camera setups for his mission of photographing Betio's coast line through the periscope, and had finally settled on a holding frame with a sequence-timing device. In

[1] It was later confirmed: *I-25* never returned to Japan.

carrying out the actual assignment on the morning of the 19th, Irvin brought the sub too close to the island; it was spotted and shelled by coastal batteries and barely escaped. The worst was yet to come. That night around ten, on the eve of the landing, *Ringgold* picked up a pip on her SG radar and quickly reported to Admiral Hill:

> Skunk [*unidentified surface target*] *bearing 278 true, distance seven miles.*

The vessel was moving south at twenty knots. All ships of the task force had been warned to keep an eye out for *Nautilus,* even though she was thought to be operating some miles to the west. Commander Irvin was expected to take her down if he chanced to encounter the Southern Attack Force. The trouble was, *Nautilus* was momentarily hung up near a dangerous reef and Irvin, very much on the horns of a dilemma, judged that it would be more hazardous to submerge than to stay where he was. Admiral Hill knew that the radar pip might well be *Nautilus* (as it was)—but it might also be an enemy patrol vessel that could give the whole show away. He gave the order to fire two salvos. At 9:59 *Ringgold* opened fire; a five-inch shell struck the submarine near the base of the conning tower, rupturing her main induction valve—but not exploding—and some thirty tons of sea water came pouring terrifyingly through the breach. Irvin took the sub down to a depth of fifty fathoms, managing to skirt the reef, while the damage-control party worked frantically to plug the hole. Within two hours *Nautilus* was shipshape enough to take up her mission where she had left off, and Irvin headed for Abemama with his wrung-out crew and his hundred wrung-out Marine passengers.

Part II:

INVASION

1

D-DAY

It was forty-five minutes after midnight, Saturday morning, when the Marine buglers sounded reveille—the last bugle call many who heard it were ever to hear. The light of a gibbous moon shone brightly over the convoy, the ships casting long shadows across the water. In the steaming galleys of the troopships, breakfast was laid out and the men began lining up for a New Zealand-style meal: eggs and coffee, potatoes and steak. Robert Sherrod heard one surgeon complain, "Steak and eggs! That'll make a nice lot of guts to have to sew up."

The *Time-Life* man had been up for a long time. The evening before, he had stuffed cans of C- and K-rations into his haversack and filled two canteens with water, hooking them onto the web belt he would wear the next day. He had also packed two morphine syrettes and a small bottle of "medicinal" brandy the surgeon had given him. It was only 8:30 p.m. when he stretched out on his rack for the night; in the darkened cabin he smoked one cigarette after another and got no sleep at all. At 11:30 he arose and climbed up to the flying bridge where it was cooler, with a brisk breeze on the rise. He was still there at reveille, when the half-moon began dodging in and out of the clouds, a moon so bright he could have written a dispatch by its light.

* * *

Colonel Shoup was up too. As a man who believed in careful preparation, he had consulted with staff officers throughout the voyage, hashing over possible situations that might arise. Whenever he found himself alone he would ask himself sudden thorny questions ("What do I do if the Japs recapture the pier?") and work out the alternatives. On the final evening he lay on his rack chewing on a succession of cigars, going over the whole thing once more. Reveille caught him by surprise.

Corporal Byron De La Beckwith (Greenwood, Miss.) was one of the amtrac machine gunners whose fighting spirit had been boosted by the addition of the armor plating. Not that his morale had been low before that; Beckwith was a happy-go-lucky youngster who, like most American servicemen, expected to survive and was doing his best to enjoy a temporary military sojourn. Perhaps the most unusual thing about him was that he considered Guadalcanal, where he had seen action, a "storybook tropical paradise" and actually planned a return visit someday. Tarawa was something else entirely; he never expressed a wish to see Betio a second time.

Beckwith was as ready as he would ever be. His most valuable possessions, a Bible and a copy of the *Rubaiyat*, were safely stowed in his pack. In the pocket of his jacket was the straight razor he intended using on any Japanese who might try to jump in the amtrac with him. Beckwith had prayed fervently the evening before, asking God to keep him from displaying any fear—he did not want his comrades to be adversely affected—and to keep him faithfully behind his machine gun no matter how stormy the weather got.

At 2:05 a.m. the last wheel was made to a course due east, in order to close the objective while it was silhouetted by the moon. Betio was sighted from the flagship bridge at 2:50 and

Julían Smith, peering through his binoculars, was able to make out a few dim lamps on the low-lying island.

At 2:55 Transport Commander Knowles reported to Admiral Hill that all sixteen transports were in position. They happened to be in the *wrong* position, but no one knew that yet. From ship to ship the thin piping of bosuns' whistles sounded and then the whine of winches, as the landing boats were lowered into the water and began circling off the stern of each troopship. Heavily laden Marines in mottled dungarees crowded the passageways, some cracking jokes or whistling cockily to cover their fear, most of them sweating in clammy silence.

A red light on the lead cruiser began blinking on and off; no one seemed to know what it meant. A calm voice came droning over the *Zeilin* loudspeaker: "Target at 112 true, 26,800 yards."

The flickering lamps Smith had seen were out now. Suddenly a powerful searchlight winked on at the northwest corner of the island and began sweeping the horizon, a vivid lance of light. It lingered for a moment on a lone transport, then snapped out. Everyone gazed across the moonlit waters at the silent dark island, waiting to see what was going to happen next.

Most of the Japanese sailors on Betio were already at their battle stations. Many wore *semin bari* around their waists; according to ancient tradition, the thousand stitches, each one sewn by a different well-wisher, gave him divine protection. Others carried a square of white silk with the Rising Sun in the center and various ideographs around it: *Prayers for your military good fortune,* or *I pray for your success in battle.* None referred to the hope of the sailor's survival, for that was not the way of the *Bushido* code in which bodily disaster was unimportant. As it was written in the Imperial Rescript to Soldiers and Sailors:

Be resolved that honor is heavier than the mountains, and death lighter than a feather.

The Japanese soldier in World War II fought—as an individual—as well and as bravely as any warrior the world has ever seen. Subject to none of the inhibitions of Western battle ethics, he was as ready to slay a corpsman tending the wounded as he was a chaplain administering last rites or even the dying man himself. As Marine historian Frank Hough observed, "What we did not realize at the outset was that we were fighting what was essentially a medieval nation, with the medieval conception of total war, total destruction."

Petty Officer Tadao Oonuki had been sitting inside his Type 97 ever since the American armada appeared on the shimmering horizon. The tank was parked beside the admiral's headquarters, and Oonuki had observed much bustling about during the early hours of the morning. Catnapping on and off, he had missed the silent drama of the searchlight; but at 4:41 a.m. a loud pop several hundred yards to the west woke him up and he saw a red star cluster blossom brilliantly over the lagoon, its placid waters reflecting the fireworks. A few minutes later the Vickers gun at the island's northwest corner loosed an eight-inch shell in a rolling boom that made him jump. The gun crew had fired at a flash that momentarily lit up one side of an American warship (it was the catapult mechanism launching the *Maryland*'s observation plane), but the shell splashed harmlessly a few hundred feet beyond. In answer, one of the other battleships swung her bow beachward and let go with a salvo, and the Marines in the bobbing Higgins boats gawked at the red blob that streaked overhead and plunged into the lagoon, short of the target.

On the island, Oonuki and his compatriots waited tensely for the next salvo. It came, a monster cluster of projectiles, one of which touched off an ammunition dump in the grassy triangle at the center of the island. For a moment Betio was blindingly illuminated; then darkness closed in again and a pulsing fire silhouetted the palm trees behind Red Beach 2.

Oonuki knew he was about to see all the combat he could handle.

Admiral Hill abruptly canceled the counterfire when he learned that the troopships were in the wrong area; in their present position they would block the ship-to-shore fire. Worse, the troopships had inadvertently been brought within range of the Vickers guns. Having driven the flagship *Maryland* farther out to sea, these guns now began shooting at the *Zeilin, Heywood* and *Middleton.* Captain McGovern was ordered to move his transport group to the proper area as fast as he could; soon the fat gray ships were lumbering southward, with the Higgins boats and amtracs plowing after them like so many ducklings. Although it was not generally recognized yet, Knowles's navigational blunder had thrown the complicated and very tight timetable completely out of whack; from this point on things were to go from bad to worse, as Hill was now forced to hold up the general pre-invasion bombardment.

The sky was beginning to lighten in the east. On the bridge of the flagship Harry Hill and J. C. Smith were impatiently scanning the skies. The planes that were supposed to deliver the pre-invasion air strike were late. Hill had no idea what had gone wrong and was unable to contact the planes or the carriers from which they had been launched—his radio operators were having unexpected and bewildering problems with the equipment. Twenty-five minutes passed as the sky took on more light and the seaborne artillery remained silent.

(How Admiral Shibasaki employed his troops during the battle of Betio remains largely a mystery to this day; historians and students of the campaign can only speculate.[1] But there is little doubt that during the lull he took the opportunity to shift troops from the oceanside to the lagoon beaches,

[1] "In terms of pertinent captured documents, the Gilberts provided far less material than was the case in many other operations. As a consequence, it is difficult to reconstruct the action from the Japanese viewpoint" (official Marine Corps history).

for it was obvious now that the invasion attempt was coming from that direction.)

Hill, deciding he could wait no longer, gave the order to begin the ship-to-shore bombardment. Just then Captain Tate, his air liaison officer, came rushing in.

"The planes are on the way!"

Hill quickly canceled the order. A few minutes later Dauntless, Avenger and Hellcat carrier planes were pouring a rain of bombs and bullets up and down the beaches. After seven minutes of this they regrouped and flew back to the carriers *Essex, Bunker Hill* and *Independence*.

It had been an impressive show, visually—but Colonel Shoup was disappointed; he thought it a puny affair compared with the aerial bombardment he had counted on. In the planning stages he had requested that Seventh Air Force drop 2,000-pound "daisy cutters" to kill the troops near the beaches and level the few wooden buildings offering concealment. The request, approved by Smith, was never fulfilled. Weeks later he found out why. A flight of twenty-four Liberators (based at Funafuti, several hundred miles to the south) had been assigned the mission; but the pilots were inexperienced and the first bomber, flown by the squadron leader, splashed into the water at the end of the runway. The next four made it safely into the air, but the one after that crashed. The rest of the pilots—eighteen in all—simply refused to take off. The four in the air attempted to carry out the mission; they dropped their bombs—but not on Betio. It has never been established what their target was. Probably Maiana.

By now it was past six o'clock and the first molten tip of the sun peered over the eastern horizon, spreading shimmering rays across the water. As far as the weather was concerned, it was obviously going to be a beautiful day. Correspondents on the lookout for irony noted that the clouds on the horizon were blood-red.

The naval bombardment began—at last—at 6:22 and continued for a deafening eighty minutes, a systematic going-over

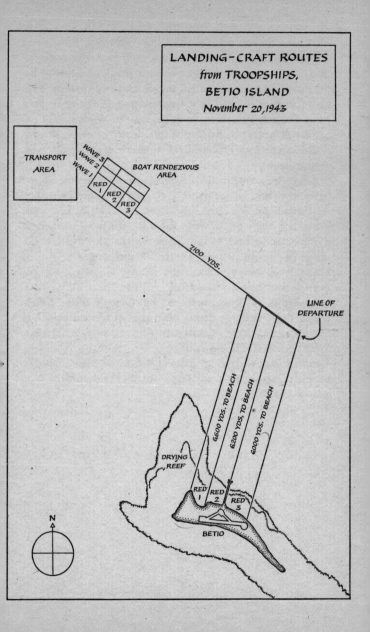

LANDING-CRAFT ROUTES
from TROOPSHIPS,
BETIO ISLAND
November 20, 1943

TRANSPORT
AREA

WAVE 3
WAVE 2
WAVE 1

BOAT RENDEZVOUS
AREA

RED 1
RED 2
RED 3

7100 YDS.

LINE OF
DEPARTURE

6600 YDS. TO BEACH
6200 YDS. TO BEACH
6000 YDS. TO BEACH

DRYING
REEF

RED 1
RED 2
RED 3

BETIO

N

of the whole island. Three battleships and four cruisers threw three thousand tons of high-explosive shells into Betio, the warships firing in salvos, drifting in and out of their own smoke as they paraded in the waters west of the atoll. This bombardment was more concentrated per square yard of ground than any pre-landing bombardment in naval history; shell fragments were later found on nearly every square yard of the island.

Almost unnoticed amid the great booming racket, an internal explosion blasted apart a gun turret on the battleship *Mississippi.* No less than forty-three American sailors were killed, and many others wounded; but such was the carnage shortly to come, both ashore and at sea, that this disaster was relegated to mere footnotage in the battle reports.

The bombardment ended, the echoes rolling out to sea. Betio looked like a smouldering volcano; great dust clouds swirled upward with smoke coiling through them, flames tinting them with a fluttering pink glow. It seemed as if Admiral Kingman might be right after all, for if ever an objective looked obliterated it was Betio.

Robert Sherrod, gazing across at the ruined island, thought to himself, "If there *are* any Japs there, they're dead now."

2

HAWKINS
AND COMPANY

When the bombardment died down Petty Officer Oonuki opened the tank's hatch cover and poked his head out. He could see very little except for a few shattered palm trees shrouded in smoke—and another Type 97 a few yards away. After some shouting back and forth, he ascertained that the other tanker had received no new orders. He called out to a third tank some distance to his left, but there was no answer. Climbing down to investigate, he went over and rapped on the hatch cover until someone opened it from inside. Oonuki looked in and gasped at what met his eye—every member of the crew was wounded. Flames from a bursting shell had flashed through the observation slits, which the driver had carelessly left open. Petty Officers Maeda and Tasukagoshi were all raw meat along their left sides; the tank captain, Petty Officer Shiraishi, was slumped in gray-faced shock.

While helping to move the wounded men into the command post, Oonuki learned that the island's main generator had been demolished in the bombardment, which meant that all wire communications between units was dead—a fact that contributed significantly to the battle's outcome. Oonuki knew, along with every other member of the garrison, that he was expected to follow the *Yogaki* Plan no matter what happened; that is, allow the enemy to approach the beach and kill him there. The thing to do now, he decided, was to move his tank closer to shore. The other driver disagreed; he said he thought it wiser to stay in his emplaced position.

The 97 would not start; Oonuki could not even get the engine to turn over. Standing up in the hatch, he waved the other tank over. After a twenty-yard push the motor sputtered to life and a great cloud of black exhaust smoke gushed forth. A moment later the U.S. destroyer *Ringgold*, having just darted boldly into the lagoon, began blasting away at the shore from close range ("... a move," said Oonuki later, "that we found most terrifying"). Several rounds landed close enough to the 97 to convince him that the enemy had seen his exhaust smoke and was trying for a knockout. He backed to a safe position in the lee of the headquarters blockhouse. Only after the shells had begun landing across the airfield did he sally forth again, pointing the clanking machine toward the western sector where there was a good view of the lagoon and the oncoming enemy.

Japanese counterfire was already beginning to build up, and *Ringgold* was having a rocky time of it. The destroyer was hit on the starboard side by a five-inch shell which penetrated the after engine room but failed to explode. It was *Ringgold*'s lucky day; seconds later another glanced off the barrel of a torpedo mount and thudded to a stop in the sick bay, also a dud. Through the breeze-blown eddies of dust and smoke, *Ringgold*'s gunnery officer spotted the flashes of the weapon doing the shooting, trained his guns on it and gave the order to fire. For the second time that morning an ammunition dump went sky-high, the five-incher destroyed by its own stockpile.

The sun was well up over the horizon now, as the three waves of amtracs crossed the line of departure and went churning toward shore in perfect order. There were forty-two amtracs in the first wave, twenty-four in the second, twenty-one in the third; with an interval of three hundred yards between waves, it was an impressive formation. The 1,464 Marines aboard were for the most part too tensely preoccupied to pay much attention to the beauty of the morning with its clear skies and soft aromatic air—air that was fast becoming polluted as the amtracs came under the drifting smoke from bombardment fires.

Lieutenant Commander Robert MacPherson, the *Maryland's* spotter pilot, had the only clear view of the action and was in constant touch with the flag bridge. Braving anti-aircraft fire, he swooped down low at one point to take a look at the reef. What he saw shocked him to the core. There was so little water on the reef that some of the coral was actually drying in the sun; the rest was awash in three feet of water or less. MacPherson, then, became the first to discover that the shallow-draft Higgins boats, even now starting to follow the amtrac waves in, were not going to be able to get across the reef. The Marines in the fourth, fifth and sixth waves were going to have to climb down into the water and wade across bullet-swept distances up to eight hundred yards.

MacPherson relayed the news to General Smith and, circling, watched as the prehistoric-monsterlike amtracs began to climb effortlessly onto the outward edge of the reef and head toward Red Beach 1, Red Beach 2, Red Beach 3. He could only hope that the amtrac-landed troops would be able to wipe out whatever Japanese had survived the bombardment, and save the others from having to make that long wade under fire.

In one of his low passes MacPherson had noticed a pair of landing craft that were laboring along several hundred yards ahead of the first wave; these, he knew, bore Lieutenant William Deane Hawkins and his Scout-Snipers. He watched as the first of the two boats came butting up against the Y-shaped seaplane ramp at the pier's lagoon end. Two men jumped onto the ramp, followed by four others, and ran onto the pier itself to find cover amid a stack of boxes.

Tarawa had been invaded at last.

The rest of Hawkins' platoon remained huddled in the two boats, awaiting his signal to follow. The signal was never given; Hawkins found that he and his five needed no help in annihilating the clusters of Japanese even now firing into the oncoming waves of amtracs. The nearest machine-gun crew was firing from inside an equipment shack near the pier's end. Lieutenant Alan Leslie (Milwaukie, Ore.), carrying a flame thrower, aimed the nozzle and squeezed out a billowing blast of orange flame; the shack and its inhabitants vanished in a fierce crackling blaze, and the Marines rushed on past. Farther down the pier, Hawkins pointed to a half-sunk motorboat resting against the pilings on the east side. Leslie loosed another rolling ball of fire, its edges sizzling as it stroked the surface of the water, and the six moved past what was now a blackened pile of burning lumber. Thirty yards farther on Hawkins motioned his men flat and lobbed a grenade at a machine-gun crew he had glimpsed on a platform among the trestles: the explosion jogged the entire end of the wooden pier. In this fashion Hawkins, Leslie and the others cleared the pier of all snipers and machine gunners, and raced back to the Higgins boats. His mission completed, Hawkins ordered the coxswains to steer both boats out into the lagoon, where the Scout-Snipers were to wait for an emptied amtrac to carry them ashore.[1]

[1] Captain Aubrey K. Edmonds, executive officer of Easy Company, 2/8, came in on the first wave and saw Japanese sailors running onto the pier from the shore end. Coming alongside the ramp, he jumped out with a few others and proceeded to do a replay of the Scout-Sniper exploit. To this day Edmonds believes that he was the first man to reach the pier and that his group did much of the work credited to Hawkins. The most plausible explanation: Hawkins' boat had already backed off when Edmonds' amtrac broke through the smoke and he got a clear view of the pier—which was once again filling up with Japanese. (That the smoke from the bombardment was thick enough to obscure vision is indicated by the presence of the mine sweeper *Pursuit* at this time, whose searchlight was being used to poke a "hole" in the smoke for the amtrac drivers to guide in on.)

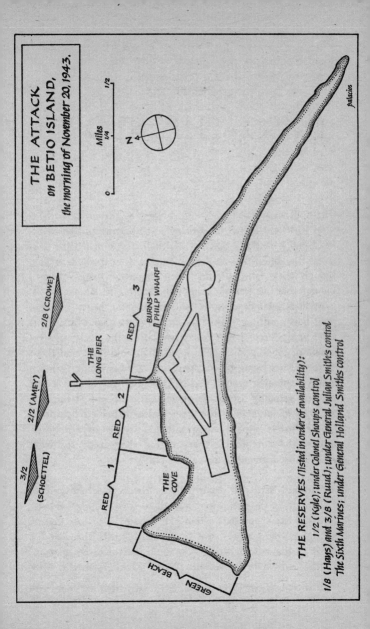

THE ATTACK
on BETIO ISLAND,
the morning of November 20, 1943.

Miles

0   1/4   1/2

N

3/2
(SCHOETTEL)

2/2 (AMEY)

2/8 (CROWE)

THE LONG PIER

RED 1

RED 2

RED 3

THE COVE

BURNS–PHILP WHARF

GREEN BEACH

Palacios

THE RESERVES (listed in order of availability):

1/2 (Kyle); under Colonel Shoup's control

1/8 (Hays) and 3/8 (Ruud); under General Julian Smith's control

The Sixth Marines; under General Holland Smith's control

3

INTO THE STORM

The amtracs were coming into range now. From three thousand yards out a kind of St. Elmo's fire began to flicker overhead and something that felt like hot sand brushed the Marines crouching low—air bursts from anti-boat shells which, though they failed to do much damage,[1] were evidence enough that this was not going to be another Kiska.

At fifteen hundred yards, bullets from the heavy machine guns began rattling against the frontal plating, and by a thousand yards most of the men were flat on the deck, as a typhoon of sound and flame erupted all around them and there were amtracs being blown apart, amtracs beginning to burn, amtracs spinning around and sinking. There were also a few amtracs grinding ashore, however, rising up out of the surf with water streaming from their sides, helmeted figures in mottled green leaping out, sprinting across the narrow beach toward the dubious sanctuary of the coconut-log sea wall, and falling, many of them, as they ran.

Corporal Beckwith manned the starboard machine gun on an amtrac in the first wave, and there was nothing between him and the enemy but a thin plate of steel. His job, that of all the amtrac gunners, was to fire short bursts ahead and a little to the left and right, hopefully keeping the enemies' heads down while the Marines poured ashore. He began firing

[1] The too-heavy explosive charges in the shells broke the casings into sand-sized and relatively harmless shrapnel.

the big fifty-caliber gun as the amtrac climbed onto the reef, five hundred yards off Red Beach 2, the center beach. The long pier stretched out on his left while, to the right, an abandoned ship of some kind loomed vaguely—Beckwith was far too busy to study either. From time to time he felt the hot, sandblast-like spray of the air bursts across his face and hands, but kept firing.

At four hundred yards out the gun jammed and he frantically tried to clear it, the amtrac crawling steadily ahead and the men on the deck yelling at him to keep firing. Rather than waste time trying to trace the trouble, he yanked the fifty from its rail mount and shouldered his way to the rear, where he exchanged it for the thirty-caliber gun that had been dangling uselessly at the stern. All this took some doing because of the press of men and gear, and by the time he had the gun mounted on the forward rail the amtrac was only two hundred yards from shore.

He began squeezing off short bursts, the gun feeling puny in his hands after the big bucking fifty; but he could plainly see the bullets kicking up sand on the beach and chipping away chunks of wood along the top of the sea wall. The men behind him yelled after every burst, encouraging him to keep it up. Beckwith, it should be noted, was the most vulnerable man in the craft, firing from a platform with his upper body exposed.

An enemy machine gunner now zeroed in on them, and bullets came plunging through the steel skin of the craft—one opening a hole directly in front of Beckwith, passing between his legs and drilling a man behind him; others went down as well. Beckwith glanced over at the driver, Corporal Ernest Hatch, and saw that he had survived the burst and was holding the vehicle in a straight line toward shore. Shore was precisely the last place Beckwith wanted to go but, conscious of the cries of shock and pain behind him, he continued pumping out brief bursts as the amtrac crawled ahead at a maddeningly slow pace.

A hundred yards from shore his luck started to run out. An

enemy gunner, possibly the same one, got off a long spray of bullets and some of them slammed into the gun-mount rail, splattering fragments of lead and steel into Beckwith's face and hands, and burring the round just entering the gun's chamber. It jammed the mechanism, and for the second time in five minutes he found himself behind a weapon that did not work.

Someone yelled, "Keep firing—keep the bastards' heads down!"

Beckwith's sense of duty was strong. He believed he was to remain erect behind the useless gun, though no one would have thought him cowardly if he had ducked down like everyone else. He felt that he could not tell them the gun was useless and incapable of keeping anyone's head down, when they themselves were about to jump onto the beach and "leap right into the mouths of the enemy's guns." It may not have been quite logical and it was not the most intelligent thing Beckwith ever did, but it was very much in the spirit of Marine Corps tradition for him to stand there—absolutely certain he was going to get shot—solely to make an ostentatious show of clearing his gun, giving his comrades at least the hope of some covering fire in the last moments of the approach.

When a rifle is fired directly at you, even from a distance, it makes a different sound than when the next man down the line is the target; the sound is sharper and seems to reach inside one's head. Marines discover this when they pull duty in the target butts at boot camp. Beckwith now heard the sound, and was not surprised to feel instantaneously a sharp pain in his left thigh ("like someone driving a hot spike all the way through"). Blood squirted out and he found himself rolling around the deck, his hands clamped over the wound.

The amtrac slowed down as Corporal Hatch yanked the levers, bringing the craft to a halt on the narrow beach itself, and the unwounded went slithering over the side.

Major Henry Drewes's amphibian tractor battalion was being wiped out all around him. He was riding in on the second wave, standing up front beside the machine gunner, and despite the death and destruction all around him he kept calling out flippant, stiff-upper-lip remarks to the others in the craft whenever a shell burst close by. Those who were watching him for moral support told correspondents later that Drewes died with a grin on his face, as a bullet drilled him clean through the brain. Everyone was glad the major had not known what hit him.

Pfc. Donald Libby (Donora, Pa.) also came in with the second wave. Machine-gun fire had been spanking clangorously against the sides of the amtrac ever since it lumbered onto the reef. As the craft drew closer to shore the bullets began to penetrate the steel; Libby was hit twice, one bullet in each thigh. A moment later a mortar shell came plummeting down and the explosion hurled him violently over the side into the water. When he floated to the surface and looked himself over, he found that one side of his body was peppered with steel fragments. He plucked out as many as he could. After that he dog-paddled weakly over to the craft, canted on its side now, and hung on, letting the motion of the surf gently rock him. The salt water seemed to stanch the flow of blood. A life preserver miraculously floated by; he grabbed it and put it on—clenching his teeth as he did so, for his wounds were beginning to stiffen up.

Libby's amtrac had been on the extreme right of his wave and he was quite isolated now, floating alone on the edge of the line of approach. Looking toward shore, he could see many men wading and hear an officer or two yelling at them to spread out. In a little while, after the pain subsided, he would try to swim out to the ships and safety. That was his plan, at least. Before he could carry it out he was to undergo an experience even more terrifying than the one he had been through in the past hour.

Corporal Beckwith was lying in the amtrac with eight or nine others, waiting for the Navy corpsman to get to him. The rest of the Marines, the able-bodied ones, had disappeared over the side to join the battle. Beckwith had seen his lieutenant pause to glance at the wounded and dead he was leaving behind, and the expression of horror on the officer's face had shocked him as much as anything. His own wound was not hurting him much and he lay quietly, plugging the hole with his hands and watching the corpsman work his way closer. He noticed how unnaturally calm everyone seemed to be; no cries of pain, no sign of panic (". . . only a few very profound curse words").

With two blasts on the air horn Corporal Hatch had backed slowly off the beach into the water, making no attempt to turn around since he wanted to keep the frontal plating between them and the enemy—even though it had done little to stop the bullets that wiped out a third of the men aboard. About a hundred yards out, an anti-boat gun got their range; the shells were like someone with a sledge hammer trying to break through, and with each blow came a shower of flying metal. One of them conked out the engine and Hatch was unable to bring it to life again.

"That's it," he yelled. "Let's hit the water!"

Beckwith, ignoring the pain that was beginning to take hold, helped the others get the more seriously wounded over the side. As they began to wade, they all came under a hail of machine-gun fire; there seemed no way of escape.

"Disperse, disperse," someone yelled.

"Disperse hell," Beckwith recalls saying. "Submerge!"

He took a breath, plunged under the surface, grabbed hold of a jagged outcrop of coral and hung on. The water was cloudy with coral dust and all he could see were his hands and the coral around them. The underwater silence astounded him after the cacophony of the battle. Some time later Beckwith found himself lying on the deck of a tank lighter far out in the lagoon, with no recollection of how he got there. Evidently a corpsman had given him a morphine injection, for he was feeling no pain at all. By nightfall he was safe aboard the hospital ship *Solace;* Byron De La Beckwith's days as a fighting Marine were over.

The statistics alone tell what happened to Drewes's amtrac battalion. Thirty-five of the tracked vehicles sank at sea, 26 filled with water on the reef, 9 burned on the beach when their gas tanks ignited, and 2 were blown up by mines. The first three waves had crossed the line of departure with 125 amtracs; only 53 made it safely to the beach. So much for the machines; the human loss was far more terrible. Of the 500-odd men who made up the amtrac crews, 323 were killed or wounded, plus Drewes himself.

The Higgins-boated fourth wave now approached the reef, the sound of the shore guns slapping hoarsely across the water at them. With a dreadful, sickening, gritty vibration, the forwardmost boat in the wave abruptly scraped bottom, and the others pulled up abreast on either side. The pilots poured fuel to their engines, but it was no use—none of the craft was able to make any further headway at all. The reef had stopped them cold, as everyone had feared it would.

The fifth and sixth waves in turn scraped to a halt. In some places the beach was as far away as eight hundred yards, and the intervening space was swept with gusts of bullets and exploding shells. All the men in the Higgins boats were going to have to wade across the reef. The bloodiest phase of the battle for Betio was about to begin.

Oonuki had found a spot that offered an excellent field of fire. He had maneuvered the 97 to a position halfway between the airplane revetments and the cove which, to those who thought Betio's shape resembled an upside-down bird, corresponded to the bird's neck. He watched as the tiny green figures moved closer through the water. To have an armed enemy coming toward you is as psychologically stunning an experience as there is, and Oonuki sat gawking for some time before he took hold of the 7.7-mm. gun and began squirting long streams of bullets across the advancing American line. He saw men fall but never knew whether he or someone else had made the hit. Nowhere could he spot a single compatriot, even though hundreds of Japanese, perfectly hidden in bunkers and blockhouses and camouflaged rifle pits, were sending forth a tremendous curtain of fire across the waters of the lagoon.

Most of the American tankers, he noticed, were trying to come ashore on the other side of the long pier and therefore did not threaten him. Two of them, however, were heading for that point of land that was the Betio bird's beak, and he threw an occasional worried glance in their direction. As the sole Japanese tanker in the immediate sector, Oonuki felt naked and vulnerable.

A series of sharp knocks on the tank's side made him jump, and he peered through the narrow slot. A sweating, out-of-breath sailor stood there banging away on the hull with the butt of his rifle. Oonuki acknowledged him by waggling the fingers of one hand through the slot; the man brought his face close and shouted that Oonuki was to drive the tank back to the admiral's headquarters right away. Oonuki wheeled the machine around and clanked off to the east, the sailor staying close on the right for protection. Oonuki had no idea how many Americans he had killed or wounded.

4

THE LANDINGS
Red 1 at 9:13

The actual beach landings—as opposed to Hawkins' pier foray—began at 9:13 a.m. when the first man from Major John Schoettel's unit (3rd Battalion, Second Marines) came splashing ashore.

Schoettel's sector was Red Beach 1, which included the cove. Two unusually large blockhouses stood athwart the imaginary dividing line between Red 1 and Red 2, and their fire now began to rake the battalion's left flank as it came in. (During the first two hours of the battle 3/2 was to lose more than a third of its men.) Fire was also sweeping across the battalion's right flank, much of it coming from the *Saida Maru*, surprisingly enough. This Japanese freighter had drifted onto the reef and foundered there after its crew abandoned it during the air strike on the 18th. The rusty barnacled wreck loomed above the wading Marines, and no one yet realized that it sheltered a number of snipers and at least one machine-gun crew. These enterprising and very bold Japanese had evidently slipped out to the freighter even as the amtracs were drawing near.

A tense and flinty-eyed young major named Michael P. Ryan (Osage City, Kan.) commanded one of the three infantry companies that made up 3/2. Coming in now on the fifth wave, it seemed from his particular vantage point that "most if not all" the amtracs in the Red 1 approach had been knocked out. He saw several men actually catch fire as two amtracs ahead of him took direct hits, and those few Marines he saw jumping out did not get far before they were blown out of the water. As Ryan crouched in the Higgins boat, he thought he heard a shout above the din of battle, and poked his head up to see his executive officer, Captain William O'Brien, yelling through cupped hands from a boat alongside.

"Major—what do you want to do?"

There was only one thing Ryan wanted to do and that was duck, but he forced himself to take another look at the beach. From the number of burning amtracs and floating Marines by the cove it seemed certain that no one was going to make it ashore there. Things looked no better straight ahead; but on the right, along the Betio bird's underbeak, he could see a few men crawling inland, low to the ground like green caterpillars. Ryan jabbed a finger in their direction. "Let's try and make it there," he shouted.

A few moments later both boats were scraping to a halt on the reef. Ryan climbed down into the water with a gut-chilling feeling of doom and, accompanied by seventeen men plus O'Brien's fifteen, began the dreaded wade-in. They had only just started when an amtrac appeared, heading out toward the lagoon. Ryan sloshed across to meet it, swung aboard and identified himself. The driver brought the vehicle to a halt and Ryan's men converged on it, glad to have an armor-plated ferry to shore; but the stationary craft drew such a sudden flurry of fire, much of it from *Saida Maru,* that they quickly backed away. Ryan and several others were already aboard, so he ordered the driver to head for the beach; but before the craft reached its top speed of seven knots it was hit squarely by an anti-boat shell and stopped in the water. Ryan and his men left the dead driver slumped over the control levers and went groggily back to their wading, their ears ringing.

Ashore at last, Ryan lay down on the sand for a moment or two to catch his breath. When he looked back toward the lagoon, it appeared to him as if very few Marines were going to reach land. He did not realize that nearly everyone had discovered the safest way to proceed was on hands and knees in the shallowing water; from Ryan's low vantage point it looked as if everyone was either wounded, dying or dead. Turning his attention inland, he quickly determined that most of the men he had seen earlier were out of action. Just as he was wondering where Major Schoettel was, a sweat-drenched private from Item Company jumped down onto the beach and told him that only forty men from that unit had survived the wade-in.

"Where's Captain Tatum?"

The Marine pointed to something resembling a beached log at the edge of the cove, water lapping lazily around it. The private had not seen hide or hair of Major Schoettel, he told Ryan; the only officer he knew to be ashore besides Ryan was Lieutenant Turner. He pointed to a sandbagged emplacement a hundred feet inland and said the officer was over there. Soon Lieutenant Samuel Turner, Item's executive officer, and Captain James W. Crain of King Company were hunkered down beside the major, filling him in on the situation. It was quickly established that Schoettel had not yet landed and that no one ashore had been able to contact him by radio.

"I'll take over," said Ryan, "until he shows up."

The others nodded, alert for orders. Ryan had assumed command of the remnant of a battalion that had left the troopships numbering about seven hundred. At the moment only a hundred or so able-bodied men were available to do battle. The battalion's mission had been to sweep straight across the island on a three-company front, but that was out of the question now. Ryan decided to try a narrow-front sweep along Green Beach instead. (Green Beach faced the open sea to the west.) If he could clear it, then reinforcements might be able to come ashore there in relative safety. He went to work organizing his stunned and scattered troops into an attacking force.

Aboard the *Maryland,* Julian Smith was waiting tensely for word from shore. His communications setup had already shown itself to be spotty at best; the battleship's radio transmitters, receivers and antennae had inadvertently been installed in such a way as to cause mutual interference. Worse, some of the equipment had got so shaken up during the naval-gunfire bombardment that it simply did not work.

One ominous message came through, however, clearly:

> *Have landed. Unusually heavy opposition.*
> *Casualties seventy per cent. Can't hold.*

No one ever identified the sender. Meanwhile Smith paced grimly back and forth on the flag bridge, pausing occasionally to take a sip of coffee or to glare through his steel-rimmed glasses toward the atoll. All he could do was try to wait patiently as the maddeningly muddled communications network sorted itself out.

5

THE LANDINGS
Red 3 at 9:17

Only one of the three assault-battalion commanders reached shore on D-day. One was killed, and the other lost his nerve.

Major Henry (Jim) Crowe, a burly redheaded man with a perpetual look of mischief in his eyes, had the least difficult time of the three—and that was true of his battalion as well. Of the 522 men of 2nd Battalion, Eighth Marines, only 25 were hit on the way in, and Red Beach 3 became the strongest of the initial lodgements. The success of their landing was due in large part to the accurate covering fire from the destroyers *Dashiell* and *Ringgold,* whose guns threw five-inch shells into the strip behind the beach just before the battalion landed at 9:17. Some of Crowe's men reported that they had found Japanese huddled in their holes face down, apparently so stunned by the rapid-fire shelling as to be virtually heedless of the Marines storming ashore.

Crowe's own journey to the beach was far from trouble-free, for he was one of the hundreds who had to wade across the reef. Bullets were splashing water all around the craft as he and his men debarked; he was surprised no one was hit as they formed a widespread line-abreast and started for the distant beach. He found himself slogging along in slow motion beside a lieutenant named Fagan. The younger man cracked a joke—something about how they could all swim out to the troopship for a coffee break if things didn't work out—and Crowe put back his head and guffawed.

"They'll have to work out *today*," he said, "and damn soon, or not at all."

Fifty yards from shore they saw three of his men get hit and go down. Crowe and those near him splashed over to a crippled amtrac that was erratically bumping its way shoreward and took cover behind it. At the point where the surf washed across the beach itself, the vehicle hit a mine and several men were knocked flat, including Crowe, but no one was hurt.

On paper, Crowe was supposed to have three rifle companies to work with: Easy and Fox companies were to advance inland on a two-company front while George Company mopped up in their wake. But Easy and Fox were not going anywhere, as Crowe soon discovered: both companies were utterly stymied by the fire from a network of fortifications on the flats beyond.

One amtrac carrying fifteen or so of Crowe's men had found a break in the sea wall wide enough to maneuver through and, churning sand furiously, had reared up and over the hummock and inland as far as the airstrip (where several Zero fighters and a couple of Mitsubishi bombers were parked). The men jumped over the sides and took up defensive positions as the amtrac rolled empty back to the beach. They were a hundred yards inland; such was the character of the battle at this point that it seemed a significant advance. But it soon became apparent that they were outflanked, and about to get cut off from the beach. In a series of backward leapfrog movements, they retreated safely before the enemy had time to gobble them up. It was a terrifying and altogether futile adventure.

The only other place where movement was possible was along the beach toward the bird's tail. Crowe's executive officer had been able to push the battalion's left flank out beyond the small wharf that once belonged to the Burns-Philp South Sea Trading Company (Sydney). Like the fifteen amtrac buckaroos who had ventured inland as far as the airstrip, these troops were pinned down and subsequently forced back. Crowe then sent George Company over to that flank, shoring it up against a counterattack that could come at any moment, and was expected to. He sent a runner downbeach in the opposite direction—toward the long pier—with orders to make contact with the Marines on Red 2. Crowe, like Ryan, had found his radios useless and was forced now to rely on messengers.

There was little more Major Crowe could do at the moment.

6

THE LANDINGS
Red 2 at 9:22

It was 2nd Battalion, Second Marines, coming in between the cove and the long pier, that encountered the worst of it.

Sometime after 9:22, when his battalion began trickling ashore, Colonel Herbert Amey (Ambler, Pa.) approached the center beach in an amtrac with his command group. Lieutenant Commander Patrick Grogan, the Navy beachmaster, later wrote down his impressions of their approach—as good a description of the unique, numbing, dreamlike terror of battle as can be found anywhere.

"It was like being completely suspended, like being under a strong anesthetic; not asleep, not even in a nightmare, just having everything stop except pain and fear and death. Everyone was afraid. No one was too proud to admit it. Our voices sounded like the voices of complete strangers, voices we had never heard before."

Colonel Amey and his group were within two hundred yards of shore when their amtrac got tangled up in a wire barricade. While the driver backed and butted and tried to break through, the colonel turned to a civilian beside him—Associated Press correspondent William Hipple—and said, "Looks like you got a story. The Japs want a scrap, all right." Then he turned around and shouted to the eighteen men behind him:

"Over the side!"

In the shallow water they all got down on hands and knees, to offer as little target as possible, and began crawling toward shore. Hipple's head was knocked back slightly; he touched his helmet, wondering what had happened: the steel was warm—a bullet had plowed a furrow in it. Bullets were zipping overhead now like swarms of giant bees. He plunged into the water, as Beckwith had done—but it was too shallow to do him much good. A few yards in front of him Colonel Amey got to his feet, raised his pistol above his head and yelled:

"Come on—these bastards can't stop us!"

An eyewitness later reported that Amey was running toward shore, his footfalls splashing up great sheets of water, when a burst of fire caught him in the chest and stomach and knocked him down. He died almost immediately.

The others waded over to one of the abandoned amtracs and huddled there, stunned. The senior officer in the group was Lieutenant Colonel Walter I. Jordan who, like Carlson, was an observer from the 4th Marine Division. Jordan knew it was his duty to take command of the battalion, at least until the executive officer showed up; there was no one else to do it. This quiet, modest officer was ill prepared psychologically for the task so abruptly thrust on him; it had not occurred to him that as a mere observer he might find himself in command of a battalion of strangers. It did not take him long to get in gear, however. In the protective lee of the amtrac he counted heads and found that of the original command group only nine remained. These he led ashore at around 10 o'clock and set up the 2/2 command post in a sand crater. In trying to contact the exec by radio, Jordan stirred up a flurry of bewilderment in the *Maryland* message center; no one knew who he was, since his name was not listed on the 2nd Marine Division roster. Jordan also tried to get in touch with the other two battalion commanders, Schoettel and Crowe, but the TBX sets had got waterlogged in the excitement on the reef and could neither transmit nor receive. Jordan had to start virtually from scratch;

he did not even know where the three companies of his newly acquired battalion were located.

As he sat in the crater trying to figure out his next move, a dusky corporal named Osbaldo Paredes (Los Angeles) came slithering over into the crater, brushed himself off, and offered his services as a runner. Jordan gratefully put him to work, and in short order the corporal was back with information that told him not only where his companies were but their strength.

The picture was not encouraging. There was no true "line"; isolated clumps of men had succeeded in thrusting themselves inland anywhere from twenty to a hundred yards from the beach, but no farther. So many lieutenants and sergeants had been hit that the chain of command was a shambles. During the wade-in so many squads and platoons had been forced by enemy fire to drift far to the right or left of their assigned landing beaches that, once ashore, the surviving officers found themselves leading men who were unknown to them. Not many had survived. Five of Easy Company's six officers were dead. One of that company's platoons had become separated during the approach and was forced to set up a defensive perimeter in a large bomb crater, where the survivors were holding off a half-circle of snipers. (It was during this action that former chaplain's assistant William C. Culp lost his life.)

The beachhead "line," if it could be called that, was more or less straight; but the disorganized 2nd Battalion, Second Marines, were cringing under such an unceasing torrent of machine-gun fire that Colonel Jordan decided to send Corporal Paredes with a desperate message to Shoup.

We need help. Situation bad.

1. Betio Island, Tarawa Atoll, September 18, 1943. Note the wide apron of reef, with fish traps and wire obstacles. CREDIT: DEFENSE DEPARTMENT PHOTO (NAVY)

2. Betio Island, Tarawa Atoll, as seen by the planes from *U.S.S. Lexington*. CREDIT: DEFENSE DEPARTMENT PHOTO (NAVY)

3. Rear Admiral Keiji Shibasaki, Tarawa garrison commander. CREDIT: WAR HIS-
TORY OFFICE, DEFENSE AGENCY, JAPAN.

4. Colonel David M. Shoup. CREDIT: DEFENSE DEPARTMENT PHOTO (MARINE CORPS)

5. First Lieutenant William D. Hawkins. CREDIT: DEFENSE DEPARTMENT PHOTO (MARINE CORPS)

6. First Lieutenant Alexander Bonnyman. CREDIT: DEFENSE DEPARTMENT PHOTO (MARINE CORPS)

7. Staff Sergeant William Bordelon. CREDIT: DEFENSE DEPARTMENT PHOTO (MARINE CORPS)

8. Machine-gun crew waiting to cross sea wall, Red Beach 2. CREDIT: DEFENSE DEPARTMENT PHOTO (MARINE CORPS)

9. Major Henry Crowe directs his battalion from a wrecked amtrac, Red Beach 3. CREDIT: DEFENSE DEPARTMENT PHOTO (MARINE CORPS)

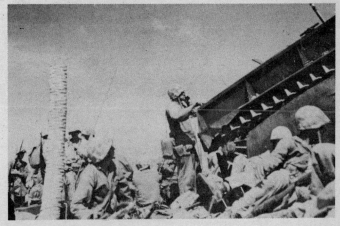

12. Marine with grenade. CREDIT: DEFENSE DEPARTMENT PHOTO (MARINE CORPS)

11. Marines advance toward the airfield. CREDIT: DEFENSE DEPARTMENT PHOTO (MARINE CORPS)

10. Crossing the sea-wall barrier. CREDIT: DEFENSE DEPARTMENT PHOTO (MARINE CORPS)

7

"... WE HAVE NOTHING LEFT TO LAND"

For many Marines on the beach, it was now time to quench their instinct of self-preservation and rise from the sand, climb over the sea wall and rush blindly inland—where heroes were sorely needed. Far fewer men did this than did not, and of those who did, far fewer survived than did not. In many cases it was necessary for sergeants and lieutenants and captains to literally kick men to their feet and shove them over the wall. Without leaders willing to bully their men into action in this manner and followers willing to fight—no matter how reluctantly—the battle of Betio would have been a defeat and a disaster.

One of the most awesome of the Betio leaders was a silent, frozen-faced sergeant named William Bordelon of 1st Battalion, 18th Marines (an engineer outfit which included the flame-thrower and demolition teams). Bordelon had ridden into battle with a platoon of twenty-two men; their amtrac was struck by shellfire when they were five hundred yards from shore, and only four men besides himself made it to dry sand. Sergeant Bordelon, infused with the spirit of attack that was so urgently needed at this moment in the battle, launched himself in a frenzy of annihilation that was to earn him, posthumously, a Medal of Honor. Riflemen covered him as he leaped across the sea-wall barrier and assaulted a pillbox alone, charging in from the flank to stuff a smoking satchel charge into the gunport. The structure erupted in a flash of somersaulting logs. Hardly pausing to catch his breath, Bordelon blasted a second pillbox apart and then a third. When he returned to the beach for another load of demolitions, a Navy corpsman noticed that the front of his dungaree jacket was blood-soaked and tried to intercept him. Bordelon waved him away, or tried to, and set about replenishing his deadly supplies. The corpsman asked him where he had been hit, but Bordelon would not answer; he was too busy for that, compulsively bent on death and destruction.

His spectacular singlehanded assaults had emboldened some of the men on that stretch of beach, and now, in threes and fours, they too ventured across the barricade. Bordelon put aside his demolition kit momentarily to cover some of them as they raced inland. The same corpsman saw Bordelon out in the surf a few minutes later, dragging a weakly spluttering man shoreward, apparently having saved him from drowning. In the final act of his short life Sergeant Bordelon climbed the sea wall with fresh satchel charges slung over his shoulder and was riddled lifeless going up against a fourth pillbox. He had been an inspiration to those who witnessed his ten-minute exploit; more and more Marines were finding it within themselves to make that most agonizing and unnatural of moves, the advance into enemy fire.

Colonel David Shoup was having a tough time getting ashore. He had held back his boat for several minutes, waiting for any amtrac that might be returning empty from the beach. Finally intercepting one, he had the wounded men it carried transferred to his boat. When that was done, he and his group —Evans Carlson among them—climbed into the tracked vehicle and headed for Red 2, the center beach, joining a cluster of tank-carrying LCMs that were chugging down the left side of the pier. A hundred yards from shore, Japanese cannon scored hits on two of the tank lighters, sinking one and forcing the other to withdraw in a sinking condition. That was enough for Shoup.

"This is no place for a command post," he said, and ordered the amtrac driver to pull back toward the lagoon. They withdrew to the end of the pier, circled around it, and headed in on the western side, between the pier and the *Saida Maru*. Halfway down the length of it the engine conked out.

"Everybody out," said Shoup, and they waded over to the shelter of the pier pilings.

His biggest problem now was the lack of communication with two of his three battalions ashore. Colonel Jordan's urgent message had been relayed to him by Jim Crowe—who had finally got a runner across to 2/2. Crowe could tell him nothing except that his battalion was solidly lodged on Red 3 but unable to move in any direction. That was the only piece of good news Shoup had, if it could be called that; he quickly relayed it out to the *Maryland*.

The only information Shoup had about the situation on Red 1 was that Major John Schoettel had not yet landed. Communications between the two officers had been poor from the start, due to a veritable epidemic of waterlogged or shot-up radios; it wasn't until 9:59 that the first message from Schoettel worked its way through the turmoil of garbles and static.

> Receiving heavy fire all along beach. Unable to land. Issue in doubt.

Eight minutes later a second message broke through the net.

Boats held up on reef of right flank Red 1. Troops receiving heavy fire in water.

Shoup responded:

Land Red Beach 2 and work west.

Schoettel's reply stunned those who heard it:

We have nothing left to land.

Shoup had one reserve battalion to work with, and now, responding to Walter Jordan's *We need help,* he sent Major Wood Kyle's 1st Battalion, Second Marines, into the battle with orders to hit the center beach and attack westward toward the embattled Marines on Red 1.

Kyle had trouble rounding up enough amtracs to ferry his unit in, and the two companies that finally headed across the reef came under such heavy fire that some of the tracked vehicles had to veer away and land on Red 1. (That was all right with Major Michael Ryan, who needed all the help he could get.) Altogether, 4 officers and 110 enlisted men from Kyle's battalion came ashore on Red 1, the rest landing on Red 2.

*   *   *

General Julian Smith, knowing he could not afford a stalemate on the beaches, had to build up Marine strength ashore very rapidly if Betio was to be conquered with a minimum of loss. Because the Sixth Marines had been given over to Kelly Turner up at Makin, Smith had only two battalions for his own (divisional) reserve: 3/8 and 1/8. At 10:18 he radioed orders that sent Major Robert Ruud's 3rd Battalion, Eighth Marines, up to the line of departure—where it would come under the tactical control of Colonel Shoup. Not yet grasping the potential disaster facing his division, he radioed Holland M. Smith at 10:36:

Successful landings on Beaches Red 2 and 3. . . . Am committing one landing team from division reserve. Still encountering strong resistance throughout.

Most of the bombardment smoke had drifted away by now, and the waters of the blue lagoon glinted pleasantly in the sunlight. Crowe's men watched as the Higgins boats of Ruud's leading wave came churning toward them, arrayed in perfect formation. The Japanese held their fire until the boats were gliding to a halt at the outer edge of the reef and the men began climbing over the side.

Clang!

The sound hurt the ears of those nearby; it sounded like an enormous steel girder falling from a height onto concrete. One of the boats had disappeared—quite literally, according to eyewitnesses. It was there, and then there was a blur and it was not.

Clang!

A second boat vanished. One of the big shore guns seemed to have found the exact and absolute range of Ruud's leading wave. After the second boat disappeared, one of the Navy coxswains lost his nerve, shouting, "This is as far as I go!" Twenty Marines piled over the side, plunging into water over their heads. Loaded down with gear, many drowned.

Shoup, watching from the comparative safety of the pier trestles, sent a message to Major Crowe:

Ruud is landing to your rear and catching hell.

Crowe did not need to be told. He and his men watched bitterly as their reinforcements were cut down in rows.

8

SHOUP'S TREK

Robert Sherrod, crouching in a Betio-bound Higgins boat, had been feeling reasonably confident until he stuck his head up for a look at the beach, still a thousand yards away. All the amtracs seemed to be wrecked or stalled or smoking. As Sherrod's boat drew closer to the beach, enemy fire began to pop and burst overhead, pieces of shrapnel dropping down all around.

"Oh, God, I'm scared," said a man beside him. "I've never been so scared in my life."

The Higgins boat scraped across the edge of the reef and ground to a halt. The fifteen Marines and Sherrod sat in stunned immobility until, a few moments later, an amtrac shuttle from the beach pulled up alongside.

"It's hell in there," the driver shouted. "I can't take you all the way in, but I'll let you out where you can wade in."

The transfer was made and the driver carried them some three hundred yards farther—while several of the men prayed openly and fervently for personal protection. Sherrod found himself trembling with fear and dread.

"From here on you'll have to wade," the driver shouted, slowing the craft down. They all slipped over the side into the lukewarm water. Sherrod later called this his "hysteria period" because, illogically, inexplicably, he was no longer afraid. He waded slowly through the increasingly bloody water with a weird feeling of calm. The sinister-looking hulk of the *Saida Maru* loomed on his right, corpses washing against its stern.

Two hundred yards from shore a movement in the water ahead caught his eye. A breechcloth-clad man, small and slender, broke surface and scrambled onto an abandoned tank, disappearing down its yawning hatch. It seemed impossible that a lone Japanese could materialize like that in an open stretch of water with hundreds of Marines all around. No one seemed to have noticed him except Sherrod. What the correspondent had seen was one of a number of daring Japanese who had swum underwater to occupy wrecked amtracs and tanks, with the intention of hiding out until they could put the abandoned rail-mounted guns to use. By noon *Saida Maru* had become a veritable fortress of resistance, although the Marines still had not caught on to that fact; the air was so dense with machine-gun fire that no one guessed it came from any direction but the island itself.

Pfc. Donald Libby was still clinging to the wrecked amtrac off Red 3, in an area where no Marines were wading. In the midst of the furious battle he was virtually alone. He had counted seven bullet and shrapnel holes in his flesh, but with the salt water stanching the seepage of blood he was not doing too badly. Swaying like a beached log in the gentle pulse of the tide, he waited patiently for someone to come for him. Around noon he spotted a man heading his way and grinned weakly, happy to see that help was coming at last. The man, wearing a Marine helmet that seemed too big for him, came splashing resolutely ahead. There was a rifle slung across his back and in his left hand a bayonet.

"What state are you from?" the man called out.

Libby was almost too late in recognizing him for what he was; his mind refused to accept it even after he saw the oriental face and heard the clumsy way the words were mouthed. Only after noticing the bayonet had a half hook at the hilt—a Japanese design for catching an opponent's bayonet and twisting the rifle out of his hands—did Libby gather himself and come to his feet unsteadily in the water. The man had already raised the bayonet to strike, and Libby threw up his hands to protect himself; the downward-arcing blade pierced the palm of his left hand but he grabbed it with his right and wrenched it away. The man fumbled jerkily with his rifle, trying to get it off his back, but Libby clubbed him behind the ear with the handle of a heavy bayonet and down he went. Libby hit him again, this time on the forehead, and held the stunned man's head underwater until he stopped thrashing.

Libby released him and, glancing back once at the body still twitching in the water, began to paddle out into the lagoon, intending to swim out to the ships. Hours later he was picked up by an amtrac crew. His body was wrinkled like a prune and blood still oozed from his hand; but he was alive and safe, and his terrifying battle of Betio was over.

The men of Ruud's battalion (3/8) were still struggling to get ashore. The water, opaque from the amtracs' churning, felt lukewarm and silky against their legs as they struggled toward the seeming safety of the beach. Every few seconds the surface would ripple and thrash as bullets came whipping across their front, and here and there men stumbled and belly-flopped ludicrously. Some rose again, while others merely rocked gently to and fro in the sun. As the survivors plodded on, soggy lumps like drowned muskrats seemed to float by on either side, clouds of blood suspended in the chalky water around them. The heads of the freshly killed bobbed on still supple necks, while the men of the first wave were already beginning to float like logs.

Overhead in the Kingfisher, Lieutenant Commander MacPherson watched the rows of tiny figures, rifles held high above their heads, falling down as in windrows, and felt hot tears of grief gathering behind his eyes.

Colonels Shoup and Carlson were still waiting among the trestles on the west side of the pier. In the water around them floated hundreds of silvery, concussion-killed fish, adding to the sickly-sweet smell of death that was already beginning to taint the air. A few of Ruud's men came wading close by the spot where the two officers stood swaying in the tide.

"Get those damn fools over here by the pier," Shoup ordered his aides, "or they'll all be killed."

The din of battle was too loud for the shouts to carry. Colonel Carlson unholstered his .45 and fired a round over their heads; that caught their attention all right, and Shoup waved them over. Carlson gathered up about twenty and started to lead them ashore.

"I'll be back," he told Shoup.

Evans Fordyce Carlson was a strange man with strange ideas. For one thing, he had a mystical concept of selflessness in battle and was convinced his survival depended on it. Only if he dedicated himself to helping others would he survive, was the way he figured it. When he first reached the pier with Shoup's party, for example, he had shucked his back pack and laid it atop a wrecked motorboat near one of the trestles. In leading Ruud's men ashore he had left the pack behind, and now, returning to Shoup, he started to retrieve it. But he stopped; it occurred to him that to do so would take him temporarily away from his task (which as he saw it was to guide more of Ruud's men ashore) and would be in a sense self-centered. Deliberately, then, he gathered up a second group and started toward the beach. Halfway along, a sniper took a shot at him and the bullet passed between his legs, leaving a painful burn on the inside of his thigh and two neat holes in his dungaree trousers. Yet his peculiar faith held fast, and he continued to shepherd groups of men ashore.

Major Robert Ruud was struggling over a tough decision. Still boated in the lagoon, he had watched his battalion being cut down in waves while from the beach came reports that only a trickle of men, exhausted and disorganized, were

stumbling ashore. Ruud did not have the authority to hold up
the remaining waves, but he did relay a vivid account of his
predicament to Colonel Elmer Hall, the regimental commander, who was stationed aboard the *Monrovia*. Whether or
not the message got through he didn't know; there was no
response for several minutes. Ruud, deciding suddenly that
he could wait no longer—for his men were continuing to die—
took it on himself to order the fourth wave to pull back into
the lagoon "for a regrouping." Soon after that the response
from Colonel Hall finally broke through—and a welcome one
it was for Ruud and those of his men who remained alive:

Land no further troops until directed.

Not so welcome, however, to the Marines ashore who were
now entirely on their own.

Colonel Shoup was watching a lieutenant climb to the top
of the pier, heading toward a wounded man who had been
crying out piteously for a drink of water; with part of his
head blown away, the man was clearly dying. Bullets whipped
across the walkway as the lieutenant crawled toward him,
canteen in hand. Shoup's high, harsh voice rang out at last:

"Get down from there! You can't waste your time on that
kind of casualty."

The lieutenant either failed to hear or ignored the order;
in any case he died sharing his water with a dying man.
Shoup, a practical fellow, was unmoved by the compassionate
but imprudent act of mercy; he knew that every lieutenant
would be worth his weight in gold this day.

Figuring now that conditions ashore could not be much
worse than they were on the reef, Shoup decided to make his
move and get a command post established in the spot where
his troops expected to find him. This final leg proved even
more troublesome than his journey to the pier. First he commandeered a Higgins boat that came up unexpectedly alongside (a narrow channel had been discovered on the west side

of the pier, deep enough for one boat) and directed the cox-
swain toward shore until such a spray of fire came against
them that he decided it would be suicide to keep going. Next
he commandeered an amtrac which he saw backing away
from shore. As he jumped aboard to talk to the driver Shoup
discovered the vehicle was filled with wounded men, or what
looked like wounded men; on closer inspection most of them
turned out to be dead. Not hesitating over the delicacy of the
matter, he ordered the crew chief and machine gunner to
help him dump the corpses over the side. That done, he
climbed back into the water and returned to the boat, where,
peering over the side, he now saw that his staff and a few
others were hugging the deck in mortal fear of the storm overhead.

"All right, who's coming with me?"

Reflecting on it years later, Shoup was still impressed that
one man—the only one out of the many in the boat—rose up
immediately:

"I'll come with you," said Evans Carlson.

The general impression among the men in Shoup's staff
was that anyone who tried to follow him ashore would be
killed; there were too many dead Marines around and too
few live ones. Shoup had given them their chance to volunteer. Now he began barking orders and calling them by name,
shaming them one by one out of their battle torpor and into
the waiting amtrac. Shoup had one more stop to make before
reaching dry land. There was a wrecked tank lighter near
the spot where the pier joined shore, and he noticed that a
cluster of men were huddled up against it, using its bulk for
cover.

"I'm Colonel Shoup," he shouted as his driver pulled alongside. "Which of you yellow sons of bitches are coming with
me?"

They looked sheepishly at him—this red-faced officer glaring down at them, erect and fully exposed to the enemy fire
which they had been hiding from. With painful reluctance,

they peeled themselves away from their precious protection and slogged toward shore.

As Shoup was crossing the beach itself on foot a few moments later, a mortar shell exploded nearby, hammering him to his knees with shrapnel wounds in his legs. Men rushed toward him, all solicitous.

"Keep away!"

He knelt there, fighting off nausea. After a minute he got up and, ignoring his wounds, began searching for an opening in the sea wall. While he was looking, his eyes fell on a pair of Marine boondockers incongruously sticking out from a pile of coral rubble. He stopped to stare. A man had crawled in there either to die or to hide—perhaps both. When Shoup saw the boondockers twitch, however, he limped over and whopped on the soles a couple of times.

"Hey, you!"

He kept it up until the fellow came wriggling out—a young corporal with coral dust all over his face.

"I'm Colonel Shoup. What's your name?"

The corporal gave his name.

"Have you got a mother back home?"

The youngster gulped, and answered bewilderedly that he had a mother back in Tennessee.

"Well, do you think she'd be proud of you, curled up in a hole like that, no damn use to anybody?"

The corporal shook his head, shamed.

"Where's your squad?" ·

He glared suddenly, eyes ablaze. "They're all dead!"

"Well, why don't you get yourself another squad?"

The corporal said he didn't know how.

"I'll tell you how." Shoup stretched out his arm toward the clusters of cowering men in mottled green along the beach. "Pick out a man, then another and another. Just say, 'Follow me.' When you've got a squad, report to me."

The corporal nodded and took off.

Shoup climbed over the sea wall and limped inland about

fifty yards, crossing a debris-strewn road that paralleled the shore. He set up his command post behind a long, low air-raid shelter with a row of shattered palm trees arching gracefully overhead. As he was getting his communications men organized—and trying to contact Crowe, Jordan and Schoettel—one of the bodyguards interrupted excitedly to tell him that the air-raid shelter was apparently filled with live Japanese.

Shoup, a busy man, merely said: "Get rid of 'em."

"We can't, Colonel—without blowing you up."

Shoup did not want to waste more time moving to another spot; there was too much rein-gathering to be done immediately. After snapping orders to have the apertures plugged up with debris, and posting sentries at the exits, Shoup settled down to fight the battle of Betio with seven or eight Japanese on the other side of the wall.

The first thing Shoup did was report his exact position to Julian Smith aboard the flagship. Smith was vastly relieved to learn that his "commander of forces ashore" had finally established a stable base of operations. The general was seen to rush over to his chief of staff and impulsively thrust out his hand.

"They've done it, Edson!"

Colonel Merritt Edson did not take the general's hand. "I'd prefer to wait, sir."

Lieutenant Colonel Presley Rixey, commanding the artillery battalion, had seen enough. His men—with pack howitzers to lug across the reef—were sure to be the slowest-moving and most conspicuous targets of all. He now ordered his boats back into the lagoon to await a more favorable opportunity; no sense trying to put guns on a beachhead that did not exist, or even on a precariously held one.

At around 11:30 several Sherman tanks came lumbering ashore, and the Marines who saw them were heartened by this dramatic show of mechanical brute strength. It was little more than show, it turned out; only four of them were able to work their way through the breach in the sea wall. One Sherman, nicknamed "Colorado" and commanded by Lieutenant Louis Largey (Hollywood, Calif.), was sent by Jim Crowe over to the Burns-Philp area on the left flank, where things were especially hot.

"Go in there and blast anything and everything," Largey was told. "Clear the way for us."

The remaining three tanks were shunted in the opposite direction to Shoup who, still in the dark about the situation on Red 1, told the drivers to keep going until they made contact with whatever of Schoettel's battalion had made it ashore. They did not get far; Marine riflemen saw the brown giants approaching and waved them back: they were afraid that shellfire from the two strongpoints at the junction of Red 1 and Red 2 would knock them out. The cannon there, in positions overlooking the cove and protected by machine guns, had driven back everything the Marines had sent against them. (These remarkable adjoining positions would remain intact and dangerous until the very close of the battle.) Shoup then directed the three tankers to spread themselves behind the ragged front held by Jordan and Kyle and to provide supporting fires for the squads even now getting ready to try and cross the taxi strip. Before the disposition could be made, one tank was knocked out by enemy fire and another got in the way of a bomb dropped from a U. S. Navy plane and was of no further use. On the left, Largey's anything-and-everything shelling was doing little to reduce the appalling volume of fire.

The tank battalion commander, Lieutenant Colonel Alexander Swenceski, had been lost early in the day when he was blown out of his amtrac—in the same manner as Pfc. Libby had been. Weak from wounds, he was in danger of drowning in water that was only a few inches deep. There were several men floating nearby, and in one spot, where the reef reached up toward the surface, four or five bodies had got entangled, making a kind of island. Swenceski crawled over to them, made certain they were dead, and flopped

down on top. All that day and night he clung to this hideous
life preserver and survived the battle he never got a chance
to fight.

Shoup could hardly have picked a worse spot for a command post. Not only was there a cluster of enemy sailors on
the other side of the wall (shouting from time to time to keep
up their courage, while trying to dig their way through), but
every so often a strafing Hellcat would chew up some sand
nearby with a burst of fifty-caliber bullets, some of which
threatened to detonate a stanchioned torpedo that happened
to be set up a few yards away. And that was by no means the
worst of it: Shoup soon discovered that he was pinned down
in a crossfire. Many of the runners who tried to approach the
command post at this time were stopped in their tracks. Shoup
began frantically trying to wave away individual men whenever they appeared out of the rubble. Already a semicircle of
corpses were fanned out around the rear of the air-raid
shelter. Shoup was so exasperated that he began throwing
chunks of coral at those who tried to approach; but in most
cases the only thing that stopped them were made-in-Japan
missiles.

One of those who succeeded in getting through was the
coral-dusted young corporal Shoup had pulled out of the burrow on the beach. He did not recognize him at first.

"I got me a squad, sir."

Shoup asked him where they were at the moment.

"In a couple of shell craters over there."

Shoup asked him if he was ready to fight.

"Yes, sir."

Shoup never did learn his name, but the corporal and his
pickup squad went on to eliminate some of the fire that had
been plaguing the command post.[1]

---

[1] When Shoup recalled this episode, dialogue and all, twenty-seven
years later, he seemed as proud of this accomplishment (turning a
scared young man into an aggressive squad leader) as anything he did
during the battle.

9

"...ISSUE IN DOUBT"

It was now noon, and the situation was critical.

Most of the amtracs had been destroyed and, owing to the failure of the tide to rise, the Higgins boats could not get across the reef. Everything was stalled; reinforcements were no longer coming ashore. Some fifteen hundred Marines were pinned down on the narrow beach, unable to advance, unable to retreat. A few hundred other bold spirits had crossed the sea-wall barrier and were engaged in killing and being killed, but the beachhead as a whole was woefully weak and scattered. No one had to be told that unless the Marines managed to fight their way off those constricted beaches they would probably be annihilated when the enemy launched his counterattack in force.

Adding to the jam-up were the swelling stacks of supplies from the transports and cargo vessels. The ship commanders, anxious to clear their holds in dangerous waters, were unloading a miscellany of equipment that bore little relation to the matériel Colonel Shoup needed. What he needed was more ammunition and water. Fuming impotently, chomping on his trademark cold cigar, he watched as amtrac crews struggled to bring ashore still more superfluous gear.

Shoup decided to send someone to General Smith and get things straightened out, and let him know what he was trying to accomplish tactically. Evans Carlson volunteered to take the message out to the *Maryland*.

"Tell him I'm trying to pull the beachheads together and push inland." Carlson nodded. "Tell him the best place to land the ammo and water is at the end of the pier. And make sure he understands that everybody ought to keep away from Red 1 and Red 3 for now—too hot there."

Carlson asked him if it was all right to delay his trip just long enough to ferry in some more of the troops along the underside of the pier. Shoup said it was a good idea. As Carlson started to crawl away, Shoup reached out and clutched his pants leg.

"Tell the general we're going to stick and fight it out."

Carlson flashed his startling snaggle-toothed grin and took off, anxious to start serving others again.

Robert Sherrod was resting beside an abandoned amtrac whose driver lay dead on the sand. With his back up against the sea wall, Sherrod felt relatively safe—until he saw two men shot as they tried to sneak downbeach to Crowe's command post, which lay just beyond the amtrac. He watched now as a third man approached, nodded a greeting, and spun suddenly to the sand with a blood-gushing hole in his head. Sherrod decided to stay right where he was, indefinitely. He heard someone yelling from the inland side of the wall:

"Major, send somebody to help me—the son of a bitch got me!"

The two men Crowe sent found a wounded Marine lying a few yards inland, and dragged him back to safety. Busy with radios and field telephones, the redheaded major happened to look up as yet another man got hit by the sniper.

"Somebody go get that bastard," he said.

Sherrod peered over the wall and watched, aghast, as a flame-thrower team flushed the Japanese from his hiding place and frazzled him to something resembling a burned frankfurter before he had run twenty yards.

Sherrod had seen that it was like a smoking city dump on the other side of the sea wall; small junk from the bombardment was everywhere—a rubber sandal, the twisted frame of a bicycle, chunks of concrete, slats and jagged planks and, strewn about, long strips of palm frond. A film of coral dust softened the edges of every object in sight, making somewhat less stark the dead where they sprawled.

Within the hour the line of side-by-side Marine corpses beside the amtrac grew in length; each man in turn had been covered with a poncho, leaving only the feet sticking out, and Sherrod found himself thinking, incongruously, "What big feet they have." At times the correspondent felt the urge to do something to help the living Marines in their desperate battle; but all he could do was sit there and watch, fulfilling the nearest thing he had to a duty by scribbling notes in a steel-backed notebook.

Early in the afternoon he caught a glimpse of William Hawkins conferring with Crowe. The fierce, attack-obsessed (and doomed) lieutenant was too busy to talk to Sherrod, but the correspondent got a close enough look at him to see that one side of his jacket was dark with coagulated blood; there was a dirty blood-soaked bandage taped against a shoulder wound. Yet he seemed to move about easily enough, and when he had concluded his business with Crowe this natural son of battle literally leaped back into the maelstrom. Sherrod never laid eyes on him again.

Hawkins was not the only wounded man doing a lot of fighting. Everyone ashore understood that the need for active combatants was enormous, and it took a drastic sort of wound to put a man down and out. A field hospital was already in operation inside one of the early-conquered pillboxes, headed by a Navy doctor named Herman Brukardt (Menominee, Mich.), assisted by three corpsmen who used flashlights to illuminate the almost ruthless surgery that saved many a Marine from death. Men needing the kind of care Brukardt was unable to provide were draped over rubber life rafts and hauled across the reef by hand, then transferred to landing boats for the trip out to the ships at sea. Often there would be dead men among the wounded by the time they reached the ships.

Sometimes a boat would be hit by Japanese gunfire on the way out. One such boat drifted alongside the *William P. Biddle* with a gaping shellhole in its hull. A boom was lowered to haul it aboard and the bodies of two Marines and a Navy doctor were all that was found inside. Chaplain Harry Boer, a newly ordained minister from Holland, Michigan, was summoned to read the last rites. Boer had never conducted a burial service before, but it didn't matter; the pallbearers and sailors within earshot were moved by the simple eloquence of his words.

"We are in the presence of the last great enemy—death. We did not know these men personally, but God knows them, and we now commit them to Him, the righteous judge of all the earth."

His words were drowned out by a long screech from shoreward as a dive bomber swooped down on Betio—then a reverberating roar as the bomb detonated the shells in still another ammunition dump. Boer continued, quoting from John, "'I am the resurrection, saith the Lord. He that believeth in me, though he were dead, yet shall he live.'" The boards were tilted, the dead consigned to the deep—to await the day when "the sea will give up its dead and there shall be no more death." Sailors lining the rail watched the place where the plunging white-shrouded figures had momentarily roiled the water.

Over a loudspeaker from the bridge came a cool report on the progress of the battle:

"The issue ashore is still in doubt."

Julian Smith was now wondering whether he ought to throw in his last reserve unit—Major Lawrence Hays's 1st Battalion, Eighth Marines, already boated and waiting at the line of departure. Most of Hays's men were eager to get into the fight; but many more were so seasick in the bobbing boats that all they wanted was to set foot on terra firma. The trouble was, if Smith inserted Hays's battalion into the battle he would then have nothing left to work with tactically; and there was sure to be a counterattack. It was 1:31 in the afternoon when, therefore, he sent an urgent message to Holland M. Smith asking him to turn the amphibious corps reserve over to his control.

> Commanding General 2nd Marine Division requests release of Combat Team 6 [*the Sixth Marines*] to 2nd Marine Division. Issue in doubt.

While awaiting the answer, Julian Smith busied himself organizing his headquarters group (staff and communications personnel, military police, medical personnel and band members) into a landing party which he planned to lead ashore in person, if his request was turned down. He knew that Holland Smith's decision on whether to release the Sixth Marines depended on how well things were going up at Makin.

In Holland Smith's opinion the Army troops at Makin were practically disgracing themselves. The flaccid fighting spirit of the 165th U. S. Infantry Regiment appalled him; their progress, such as it was, had so far been overcautious to the point of timidity. What they needed, he was convinced, was not the assistance of the Sixth Marines (which Admiral Turner seemed all too ready to offer them)—the GIs already outnumbered the enemy on Makin eight to one—but bolder leadership. Smith was just getting ready to go ashore himself and try and light a fire under Ralph Smith, the Army commander, when a sailor from the radio shack handed him J. C. Smith's message from Tarawa.

Until that moment he had not understood the gravity of the situation on Betio. The initial report, after all, had been encouraging (*Successful landings on Beaches Red 2 and*

3 . . .). He hurried over to the admiral's cabin. Turner was taking a nap; the Marine general shook him awake and showed him the message. Kelly Turner brooded over it for a moment or two, then told him to go ahead and do whatever he thought best. Smith stepped into the radio shack and issued combat orders to the commanding officer of the Sixth, Colonel Maurice Holmes, and then sent word to J. C. Smith that the fresh regiment was on its way. Ironically, that was the sum total of Holland Smith's contribution to the Tarawa phase (i.e., the Marine phase) of Operation *Galvanic*.

While he was waiting for his answer from up north, Julian Smith had sent a query to Colonel Shoup on Betio:

> *Do you consider a night landing by LT 1/8 practicable on Beach Green? If not, can reinforcements land on Beaches Red 2 and 3 after dark?*

Shoup never got the message, and Major Hays's men remained boated and hung up at the line of departure. By now they were seething with frustration, anxious to join the battle and do their share. A bit later Smith signaled Hays to land his battalion on the lagoon-side shore of the Betio tail and attack toward Crowe's enclave. This message also failed to get through, which was just as well for the six hundred men of the battalion: the narrow tapering tail may have looked deserted to Lieutenant Commander MacPherson from his Kingfisher (as he had reported), but the defenses in that sector were as formidable as any on the island.

OONUKI'S
ORDEAL BEGINS

Oonuki had driven the 97 back to Admiral Shibasaki's head-quarters, as ordered. Inside the huge compartmented shelter, his commanding officer informed Oonuki that his tank plus one other were the only two still landworthy. They were to be "the admiral's eyes," the officer explained, now that the command post was out of touch with outlying defense units. Oonuki went outside to round up his crew—but they had disappeared and he could not find them. Petty Officer Shiraishi, still shaken from the blast that had scorched him and his crew early that morning, volunteered to go along; another sailor named Ota volunteered as well.

They climbed into the tank and headed down the main airstrip; it was pocked with shell craters, and the tank bobbled along like a string-pulled toy as Oonuki, at the controls, worked his way along. The tank's heavy fuel began sloshing around and the engine cut out intermittently, sputtering. As Oonuki struggled to keep the tank alive, Ota spotted a skirmish line of Marines (from Jordan's or Kyle's battalions) racing across the taxi strip a short distance ahead of them. Ota fired a succession of 37-mm. shells while Shiraishi pumped a few bursts after them with the machine gun.

The engine finally sputtered out, and Oonuki frantically

worked to get it going again; he was sure that the enemy must be surrounding them by now, stranded as the 97 was, wholly without cover in a terrifyingly conspicuous location. Ota and Shiraishi kept firing, as Oonuki tried again and again to start the engine. The Marines had long since taken cover on the other side of the airstrip, but the two Japanese gunners continued spraying the area where they had last been seen. The tank's ammunition was nearly gone and Oonuki was about to pass the word to abandon ship, when the engine coughed and roared to life. He swung the tank around and began to creep back toward the command post in low gear: the clutch had burned out and the 97 was little more now than a large, slow-moving target.

At the admiral's blockhouse Oonuki was surprised to see so many wounded men lined up against the south wall. He and Ota helped to carry some of them inside, and afterward Oonuki, dripping with sweat, sat in the interior of the echoing, lantern- and candle-illuminated shelter, watching as officers darted to and fro, collecting stacks of papers to be burned outside. At one point a captain appeared in their midst and shouted for attention. He held a message blank in his hand, on which he claimed a radioman had scribbled a message from the Emperor himself. Everyone stiffened in awe. The officer read the message aloud:

> *"You have all fought gallantly. May you continue to fight to the death. Banzai!"*

He strode away, disappearing down one of the murky passageways. Not until much later did Oonuki come to suspect that the message was a fake, designed to lift everyone's spirits—yet he was never sure.

Matters inside the great bunker were turning decidedly melodramatic. Petty Officer Shiraishi now burst wild-eyed into the shelter brandishing a bloody samurai sword.

"I've just killed a dozen Americans," he screamed. He said he was going out to kill a few more and wanted to know who would come with him. Several men rose and followed him outside. Oonuki never saw any of them again.

There were at least three hundred men inside the shelter by this time. A high-ranking officer appeared late in the afternoon and divided them into two groups; half were assigned to Admiral Shibasaki, the rest to his chief of staff. Oonuki was in the latter group, which had the task of creating a diversion so the admiral could move to a new command post near the ocean shore. A skeletal headquarters had already been set up there and only awaited his arrival. From this spot he planned to rally the scattered groups for a general counterattack and push the Americans back into the lagoon.

Oonuki and two others again climbed into the crippled 97 and headed down the familiar airstrip. Rolling along slowly, they fired the last of their ammunition into the American-occupied strip along the airfield's northern edge. The engine gave out once again, and Oonuki knew it would be foolish to sit there indefinitely trying to restart it; he told the other two men to get outside. While they were climbing out the hatch, Oonuki went in the opposite direction, diving downward to wrench open the fuel valve and flood the bottom. As soon as the fuel was flowing he followed the others out the hatch, intending to drop a grenade in from outside; but before his feet touched the sand he was rocked by an explosion close by, and he saw the body of a man fall back to earth from what seemed a great height. Oonuki forgot all about scuttling the tank and dived for the nearest foxhole, only to find it filled to capacity with dead men. He ran farther and ducked into a hospital dugout. Maeda and Tasukagoshi (who along with Shiraishi had been scorched in their tank that morning) were huddled in there with six others, two of whom were dead.

"Kill me, Tadao," pleaded Maeda, leaning over to whisper it in Oonuki's ear. "Please kill me."

Every one of them was in bad shape, or so it seemed to Oonuki. In the dim light the six living men seemed as grotesque as the dead ones, and he found that he was a little

13. Marines moving up to assault an enemy position (sandhill in center of picture).
CREDIT: DEFENSE DEPARTMENT PHOTO (MARINE CORPS)

14. Marine squad crouches behind a bombproof, as smoke from oil fires darkens horizon. CREDIT: DEFENSE DEPARTMENT PHOTO (MARINE CORPS)

15. Colonel Shoup (center, holding map case) and Colonel Carlson (seated, front) at command post near Red Beach 2. CREDIT: DEFENSE DEPARTMENT PHOTO (MARINE CORPS)

16. Two Tarawa defenders who killed themselves as Marines approached their bunker. CREDIT: DEFENSE DEPARTMENT PHOTO (MARINE CORPS)

17. Aerial shot of Betio "tail," showing results of bombardment. (Picture taken during battle; Marines had not yet reached this area.) CREDIT: DEFENSE DEPARTMENT PHOTO (MARINE CORPS)

18. Marines assault last enemy strongpoint in Pocket. CREDIT: DEFENSE DEPART-
MENT (MARINE CORPS)

19. Shibasaki's command post, Type 97 tank beside it. CREDIT: DEFENSE DEPARTMENT PHOTO (MARINE CORPS)

22. Major Generals Holland M. Smith and Julian C. Smith after the battle. CREDIT: DEFENSE DEPARTMENT PHOTO (MARINE CORPS)

23. Generals J. C. Smith and D. M. Shoup with Robert Sherrod at 1959 reunion of Tarawa survivors, Alexandria, Virginia. CREDIT: DEFENSE DEPARTMENT PHOTO (MARINE CORPS)

20. Prisoners in temporary holding pen. CREDIT: DEFENSE DEPARTMENT PHOTO (MARINE CORPS)

21. Prisoners at end of pier, awaiting transportation to prison ship. CREDIT: DEFENSE DEPARTMENT PHOTO (MARINE CORPS)

afraid of them. Ignoring Maeda, he took stock of his food and water supply. He had started out the day with three *go* in his canteen, about one pint, but that was long gone. During the hectic morning he had lost the ration bag every sailor on Betio was supposed to keep slung from the hip; the only thing Oonuki had left was a vitamin syrette. This he now passed around, and each man squeezed a small bit onto his tongue. One of them began clawing into the sand floor with his fingers, digging down until the hole began to fill with water. It was salty and brackish, but they all got down on their hands and knees and sucked greedily at the soupy puddle.

A little later the Americans began to assault the strongpoints close by, and the seven Japanese sat listening to the explosions and the terrifying *whoosh* of flame throwers. There was a ventilation shaft in the roof of the dugout—unnoticed until a scraping sound came through it, followed by a clunk.

"Grenades!" shouted Tasukagoshi.

They snatched up a blanket and stuffed it into the lower end of the shaft. There was a muffled explosion. The only thing they could do now was wait; to try and escape by running outside would be even more hazardous, for the Americans were all around them with their rifles and grenades and, more dreadful still, their flame throwers.

All at once Oonuki felt exhausted. He leaned against the sandbag wall and slid down it, the strength draining out of him. The next thing he knew, a roaring orange hell of fire filled the inside of the dugout and he heard human voices shrieking in his ear—then oblivion.

11

THE TOEHOLD
AT SUNDOWN

Twice during the afternoon it seemed as if the Japanese were about to launch their counterattack. On Red 3, just after Marine crews had manhandled two 37-mm. guns across the reef, Crowe's men spotted the mustard-colored shapes of two tanks moving through the fantastic chaos of wreckage in the island's center, plunging side by side toward the Marine lines. Meanwhile the gun crews on the beach were trying to figure out how to get the weapons over the sea wall, and when the tanks' approach was reported to the battery commander he responded with what seemed like an unreasonable order.

"Lift 'em over!"

The crewmen grabbed hold and, unreasonable or not, the 900-pound weapons virtually soared into shooting position on the inland side of the log barrier. Putting them into action, the gunners knocked out one tank and soon had the other fleeing for its life. A little later the Marines in the same sector spotted a group of two hundred or so Japanese moving up through the sparse brush that fringed the south shore. The

37-mm. gunners opened up with canister shot and the Japanese dispersed, leaving dead and wounded behind.

The big blow was yet to come.

All afternoon the Marines had been busy smashing enemy strongpoints one by one. In a routine someone called the blowtorch and corkscrew method, engineer teams with flame throwers, satchel charges and bangalore torpedoes joined riflemen in pushing the lines ahead a few yards at a time. At that rate it was going to take weeks to conquer Betio; but the ships could not afford to play sitting duck that long. Admiral Hill's pilots had not yet spotted any sign of Koga's Combined Fleet, but its arrival was going to surprise no one.

There was nothing Hill or Smith could do to spur on the men ashore. Kyle and Jordan (1/2 and 2/2) were making some small progress inland from their center beachhead. Crowe and Ruud (2/8 and 3/8) were barely holding their own on the left, and not moving at all. On the right, 3/2 was still a question mark; for all Hill and Smith knew, Schoettel's battalion was a dead loss.

Major John Fred Schoettel, a prematurely bald, athletic-looking man from Lima, Ohio, was having the worst day of his life—one that was to haunt him for the few short months he had left. All morning Schoettel had been struggling with a profound personal problem: the fear of death. Worse, he feared for the lives of the three hundred Marines he had not yet sent ashore. Too many men of his battalion were floating face down in the lagoon as it was; he simply could not bring himself to send in the fourth and fifth waves. Not that he had the authority to hold them back—but he had done so anyway. Schoettel's radio equipment was out of order and he was not even able to maintain contact with his company commanders. Judging by the pathetic dribble of men he had seen crawling ashore, it seemed entirely possible that his first three waves had been wiped out. To cross that reef now, he reasoned, would only mean more dead Marines—and possibly a dead battalion commander as well.

Noon came and went and, as the glaring day wore on, Schoettel hovered in his boat a thousand yards offshore in an agony of guilt and doubt, refusing to give the order that would send his last two waves across that dead man's reef. Midway through the afternoon he was able to make a small contribution when he noticed two tank lighters turning away as though giving up their attempts to put their loads ashore. He intercepted them at about eight hundred yards out and ordered the ramps lowered; the tanks started in through water that threatened to drown out the engines, while reconnaissance men waded ahead of them, marking potholes in the coral with flag buoys. But the tankers found the shore line so jammed with dead and wounded that they were forced into a laborious end-around in order to cross Green Beach. Only two of the original six made it; the others were either knocked out by enemy guns or hopelessly stalled in the water.

After dealing with the tank boats Schoettel returned to the lagoon, raised Colonel Shoup at last on the radio, and admitted that he had lost contact with his troops ashore. Before Shoup could respond to this forlorn message, General Julian Smith interposed one of his own from the battleship, revealing his impatience with a battalion commander he assumed was only overcautious—rather than demoralized.

> *Direct you land at any cost, regain control of your battalion and continue the attack.*

Major Schoettel eventually showed up in the center beach sector where he reported to Shoup, explaining somewhat lamely that he had got separated from his waves out on the reef. The colonel had no troops to turn over to him—Ruud and Kyle had sucked up most of the stragglers by now. Schoettel hung around the command post for a while, very much at loose ends—a battalion commander without a command.

The situation on Red 1 was not nearly so dire as Schoettel—or Shoup—assumed. Michael Ryan was rapidly building up a strike force; a conglomerate outfit, it combined the remnants of four infantry companies plus survivors from the amtrac battalion and a handful of men from regimental headquarters. Though he had managed to corral about 250 able-bodied men, he still lacked fire support—no howitzers or mortars, no air or naval gunfire liaison to work with. It was therefore regarded as something of a godsend when the two tanks Schoettel had shepherded toward shore put in an appearance.

Ryan immediately gave orders for Item and Love companies to attack down Green Beach with the tanks in support —and a lot of men said what they thought were going to be their last prayers. But enemy resistance turned out to be unexpectedly light, as the two-abreast companies rolled up the western shore (the bird's beak and forehead), clearing that strip so that reinforcements could land there later. One of the tanks was knocked out during the push, and as Lieutenant Ed Bale in "China Gal" came up, the same gun fired again, ruining Bale's 75-mm. cannon with a glancing hit. It was a sore loss to Major Ryan, now once again without hard support of any kind.

Halfway down Green, at the point where a road from the airfield crossed to the beach, a hailstorm of enemy fire slowed the attack down to a crawl. More ominously, Ryan began to spot groups of Japanese running along his inland flank, threatening the rear of his battalion. If 3/2 got cut off from the landing beach, there would be no way to rescue them. It was late in the afternoon when Ryan's men reached the trenchlike tank trap three-quarters of the way down Green—a far deeper penetration than any of the five battalions ashore had made. The only trouble was, Japanese in growing numbers kept popping up in the by-passed areas. (Ryan's own command

post, an abandoned coast-defense gun turret, was attacked
while he and O'Brien were rounding up stragglers back on
Red 1.) Ryan's Marines had overrun pillboxes and gun turrets
with small arms but without flame throwers or heavy demolitions—which were necessary for scouring out the insides of
the captured positions. The surviving Japanese merely lay
doggo, awaiting the opportunity to strike back; and after their
positions were by-passed, many of them came to the surface
to prey on the stream of stretcher-bearers, wounded men and
ammo carriers heading back toward Red 1. One wounded
Marine was known to have been killed when his stretcher-
bearers set him down momentarily to hunt one of these
snipers.

The sand darkened as if rain was threatening; some of
Ryan's men glanced upward. It was smoke overhead, not
rain clouds—the wind had changed. Through a patch in the
smoke one could see that the sky was no longer blue; day was
fading fast over Tarawa Atoll.

With great reluctance and a gnawing sense of frustration,
Ryan decided to order his troops to fall back. They had
overrun an area that was roughly five hundred yards deep
and a hundred and fifty yards wide; but there was no telling
how many Japanese lurked in the wreckage behind them—
and that was the problem: Ryan felt that the battalion was
simply in too vulnerable a spot. One by one, then, the company commanders were told to move their troops all the way
back to the bird's beak, there to coil themselves into a tight
perimeter, the better prepared to hold out through the night.

The sky was fast darkening when the first word got through
to Ryan from Colonel Shoup, via a sweat-drenched runner
(who seemed to Ryan almost like a creature from another
world—so long had they been isolated from the rest of the
division). Colonel Shoup wanted a situation report; Ryan told
the runner to tell him that 3/2 was holding a defensive perimeter about three hundred yards from the northwest tip of

the island. That was all; he did not mention the spectacular gains he had made during the afternoon. The runner took off in the gathering gloom, heading down the body-strewn beach. He was never seen again, and the wonder of it is that he succeeded in getting through the first time, for between Ryan and Shoup lay six hundred yards of enemy territory that included the most formidable of all the Japanese positions—the two bristling gun bunkers overlooking the cove.

Lawrence Hays's floating battalion had a brief scare as dusk fell, when an unidentified plane appeared over the transport area. Tracers from the ships' anti-aircraft guns quickly chalked the sky with pastel streaks. Many of the men in the Higgins boats thought they were going to be strafed, and got ready to jump into the water. A few sharks had been spotted swishing around the lagoon, attracted by the gallons of gore; jumping over the side was therefore not something anyone was anxious to do.

But the plane was U. S. Navy. Lieutenant Commander Jesse Cook and Ensign G. K. French had been launched in a Kingfisher at 4 p.m., with orders to scout for any oncoming Japanese vessels. At 6:30, with nothing more to report than an unbroken vista of seascape, Cook requested to be taken back aboard the *Maryland.* Permission was surprisingly denied; he was told that the fleet was expecting an air attack. Some time later, no attack having materialized, he headed back toward the flagship, flying at three hundred feet off the surface. The fleet, still poised to repulse an air attack, assumed the Kingfisher was unfriendly and Admiral Hill, an officer not given to hesitation in such matters, messaged, *Open fire.*

The gunnery was erratic and the Kingfisher, as lucky as *Nautilus* had been earlier that day, escaped. Cook put the plane down on the water, identified himself, and requested a cease fire. This was granted. Admiral Hill made an entry in his log to the effect that the fleet had fired on "an imaginary target" at 6:38 p.m.—in 1943 the U. S. Navy was not ready to

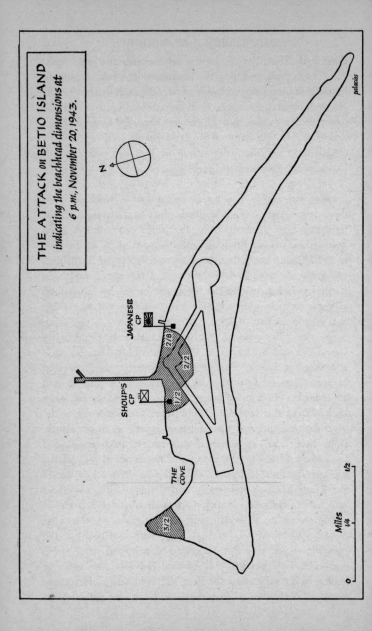

THE ATTACK on BETIO ISLAND
indicating the beachhead dimensions at
6 p.m., November 20, 1943.

Z

palazás

JAPANESE CP

2/8

2/2

1/2

SHOUP'S CP

THE
COVE

3/2

Miles
0   1/4   1/2

admit that friendly planes were sometimes fired on. Cook and French, stranded now by darkness, prepared to spend the night in a bobbing cork of a plane, miles out to sea.

At 7:11 p.m. General J. C. Smith signaled Shoup that he was to:

> Hold what you have. Develop contact between Landing Teams. Clear hostile machine guns still holding out on beach. Make provisions to meet organized night counter-attack. . . .

The dust had finally settled on the evening of November 20th, 1943—the longest day in the lives of those Marines, Japanese sailors and Korean laborers who survived, and the shortest for those who had not. The men of the 2nd Marine Division had tentative posséssion of two small enclaves on Betio Island; one was Major Ryan's, and the other fanned out shallowly from the base of the long pier. There were no lines as such. Crowe's men and Ruud's remnant had managed to nail down a fairly solid position on the left, but they were hard up against the enemy entrenchments. This meant that when the counterattack came it would come suddenly and without warning, for the enemy had no open ground to cross.

What the Marines had won, in a day of dreadful carnage, was less than one tenth of a square mile of coral, much of it blown to powder, much of it stained with blood. The rest of the tiny island was held by desperate men who were not only willing but positively eager to die for the Emperor—to dwell eternally at the warriors' shrine at Yasakuni.

Part III:

BREAKING
THE
STALEMATE

1

THE STORY
AT MAKIN

Things were bogged down to the north as well.

The Makin phase of *Galvanic* had begun brilliantly. Historian Samuel Eliot Morison watched the pre-invasion bombardment from the bridge of a cruiser and described the whole panorama later in these words: "The spectacular trade-wind clouds scurrying to leeward, the flash and rumble of great ordnance seemed more appropriate to the harsh crags of Morven than to this soft Micronesian dream world." Almost blithely he went on to compare the assault itself to a horse race, with two destroyers defining the starting post or line of departure. At 8:13 a.m., he reported, the chief signalman snapped a blue flag downward and the first wave of amtracs went galloping across the line, each craft trailing a long white wake "like the tail of a charger."

"There is nothing more beautiful in war," he concluded, "than an amphibious operation when it clicks; and this one did."

It was only after the Army troops actually landed that things started to go awry. No one could find any Japanese. The Butaritari natives[1] were everywhere, and embarrassingly

[1] The action took place on Butaritari Island of Makin Atoll, but the battle is usually referred to as "Makin"—just as the fighting on Betio is known today as "Tarawa."

friendly. (A marine observer, Lieutenant Colonel James Roosevelt, the President's son, who had been with Carlson in the '42 raid, was greeted vociferously and nearly mobbed.)

But where were the Japanese?

A Navy carrier plane flying down the island's length reported at 8:55 that he had seen "only desolation." Some of the officers on flagship *Pennsylvania*'s bridge expressed relief that the enemy seemed to have escaped once again, as they had at Kiska. One officer actually suggested that the final phase of the bombardment should be canceled as a waste of ammunition. Admiral Turner scoffed at this.

"I didn't come all this way," he said, "just to call off the whole thing on the say-so of one aviator."

Makin was defended by 284 men of the Special Naval Landing Force, commanded by a junior grade lieutenant named Seizo Ishikawa. There were also 100 marooned aviation personnel, 138 men from the 111th Pioneers and a construction unit consisting of 76 Japanese and 200 Koreans. All the Japanese float planes had escaped but one, a disabled bomber of the Emily type, whose crew of nine draped themselves neatly on the wings and committed ritual suicide as the American amtracs churned ashore.

The principal Japanese defenses lay halfway between two tank traps that cut across the narrow island. Several hundred GIs of the 165th Infantry were advancing slowly along a taro-plantation road leading toward the first of these traps when an enemy machine gunner and a handful of riflemen stopped them in their tracks with a tentative flurry of fire. The hours began to roll by, with the invasion inexplicably stalled. (It was at this point that Holland Smith began to get disgusted.) There were several U. S. Army tanks present which might have spearheaded an attack, but their drivers said they would take orders from no one beside their commanding officer—who was back on the beach. Colonel Gardner Conroy, the regimental commander, walked forward with Colonel Roosevelt, intending to appeal personally to the tankers to go ahead and blast the absurdly small knot of Japanese who were holding up his entire unit. He was killed by a sniper. There was no further movement that day.

Just before sunset the Northern Attack Force, hovering twenty miles southeast of Makin Atoll, half-masted its colors while the battleship *Mississippi* buried her dead at sea: the forty-three sailors who had been killed in a turret explosion that morning. The sun went down over Makin at 6:10, the sea turning the color of imperial purple for a long, dramatic moment afterward.

2

BETIO
The First Night

At around nine o'clock a fresh breeze sprang up, carrying some of the island's stink out to sea. Hundreds of corpses, having simmered in the sun all day, exuded a smell that was becoming an all-pervading presence befouling every breath a man took. It was so strong that the Marines of Hays's 1/8 could detect it a thousand yards offshore. Slated as they were for a dawn landing, it did nothing for their peace of mind.

Everything was relatively quiet for several hours; the moon rose just before one o'clock, and if one didn't look around too carefully, it was all very much a South Sea paradise, Hollywood version.

Julian Smith had sent his assistant division commander ashore for an eyewitness report on the tactical situation, but that officer, Brigadier General Leo Hermle, had got hung up at the lagoon end of the pier, trapped and isolated by the gunfire that crisscrossed its length. Eventually two of his party were able to sneak ashore, returning later to report that Shoup still needed ammunition and water, primarily, and that he wanted Hays's 1/8 to land on the center beach at dawn.

Meanwhile Smith had got off a message instructing Hermle

to *take over* the command of the forces ashore; but this message—like so many in the past twenty-four hours—never got through, and David Shoup was to retain control for another day.

General Smith was by now sorely displeased at Hermle's radio silence. As messages from the landing-force headquarters continued to bear Shoup's signature, the general became increasingly irked. When at last Hermle re-established contact at 4:10 a.m.—from *Ringgold's* radio shack—the following curt reply came bouncing back:

Report to commanding general immediately.

Arriving at the battleship some time later, Hermle was hauled aboard in a breeches buoy to find Smith awaiting him with a stern look on his ordinarily bland face. Like a father whose son has stayed out all night, the general was relieved to see his assistant but was also angry at him for getting "lost." Nor was Smith pleased that the only message Hermle brought was that Shoup needed ammo and water; Evans Carlson had brought the same message hours ago. (Carlson had, incidentally, also remarked to the general that the fighting on Betio was "the damnedest I've seen in thirty years in this business.")

The sailors on the ships had been listening throughout the night for sounds that signaled a counterattack. They listened in vain. Amazingly, the only counterattack came from the air, and it was ineffectual.

Lieutenant Commander Cook and Ensign French were dozing in their plane some twenty-five miles west of the atoll when, half an hour before dawn, a formation of torpedo bombers appeared overhead. French counted sixteen of them. One suddenly peeled off to take a closer look at the floating Kingfisher. Cook and French sat tensely, their canopy thrown back, both men poised to leap out into the water. But the enemy plane only circled once and climbed away to rejoin the eastbound formation.

Admiral Hill, now warned of the enemy's approach, ordered his picket ships to fire at random and act as decoys; but the Japanese pilots ignored them and flew straight across Betio, dropping three sticks of bombs that caused the smouldering fires to flare up momentarily. Every bomb landed in Japanese-held territory; the Marines were as amused by that as the Betio garrison had been by the inept U.S. raids in August and September.

In the waning hours of the night Dr. Brukardt's wading corpsmen found fewer and fewer bodies from which to strip first-aid kits, and by the time the first faint glow appeared in the east, there were none at all. The tide had floated them out to sea.

3

1/8

Into the Storm

Dawn was just breaking; one pale star lingered in the west, but the night was over. Here and there individual Marines lay sound asleep among the corpses—and perhaps some of them were dreaming nightmares about the counterattack that never came. Big tumbleweeds of oily smoke were still drifting across the skyline, but there was no shooting going on at the moment. Now the top of the sun peered over the horizon, staining the surface of the lagoon a fiery red. The awful business of the day was about to commence.

David Shoup had managed to snatch a catnap or two during the night; some of the officers at the command post had chuckled to see him snoring away with the cold stogie stuck in the side of his mouth. Shoup was up and about at dawn of course, and someone saw him gloomily counting the corpses that were hanging so pathetically in the barbed wire, plus the sacklike objects half buried in the sand of the beach. Around the command post itself were "bizarre red patterns"—as he later called them—made by the thrashings of men who had bled and died in the sand the day before.

Suddenly a Japanese sailor came staggering around the corner of the air-raid shelter, and Shoup snatched up his .45. But the man was harmless; wounded in the shoulder, his deltoid muscle lay open to view as in an anatomy class. Shoup grabbed the man as he started to stumble past, made him lie down on the spot, and gave him a slug of brandy from his canteen. Somehow killing him had not seemed quite the appropriate thing to do.

*   *   *

When the men of Lawrence Hays's battalion hit the reef at 6:15 a.m. they found themselves facing the same long wade that Kyle's and Ruud's men had faced the day before. Everyone fervently hoped, of course, that enough of the enemy gun positions had been destroyed that the battalion could get ashore safely; but it was not to be. The morning of the second day turned out to be even bloodier than the first—as the machine guns aboard the *Saida Maru* resumed their terrible drumming and the anti-boat guns ashore once again found the range.

In a short time Robert Sherrod had counted a hundred fresh bodies on the drying reef. Evans Carlson, stranded temporarily at the end of the pier on his return trip, estimated that he saw a hundred men get hit in less than a minute. Ashore there were groans and shouts of rage, as the Marines of the thinly held line watched their would-be reinforcements go down almost in serried ranks. There were no foxholes on the reef; one of the survivors said it was like being in the middle of a giant pocketless pool table.

The tide was out now and the enemy's bullets, instead of kicking up sprays of water, spanged off the coral and went whining into space, or else with a sickening *thwack* found flesh. Off Red 1, two Marines inadvertently wandered away from their formation and found themselves stranded on a level stretch of the reef; it seemed to observers that at least half a dozen machine guns had begun powdering up the coral around them.

"Don't move," an officer yelled above the racket. "Act like you're dead!"

The two went limp and mimicked death so realistically that some of their comrades, plodding toward shore, threw worried glances over their shoulders. Both men survived to tell about it; the same cannot be said of most of the men in their unit, however. The rest of the platoon, in trying to veer over toward Ryan's sector, came ashore in the cove and were wiped out almost to a man by up-close fire from the two blockhouses there.

Of the 199 men in Hays's first wave, only 90 made it to the beach.

Hoping to offset the fire that was mowing down his reinforcements, Shoup now directed all units ashore to attack inland with all force and speed. Lieutenant Hawkins led his Scout-Snipers in a series of assaults that ran parallel to the beach, and succeeded in forcing his way a hundred and fifty yards into the forbidden zone near the cove—later characterized by journalists as "the Pocket." The sense of urgency was tremendous; everyone was caught up in the mood. A Marine correspondent named Richard Johnston watched a spindly private crawl down over the sea wall to get himself patched up enough to stay in the fight. One of the young man's ears and half of his face were lacerated and bleeding; Johnston watched as he crouched down beside the corpsmen and waited patiently, dazed and trembling, until someone tied a sulpha bandage around his head and gave him a drink of water. He began to gather his somewhat rubbery legs under him.

"Better lie down," warned the corpsman.

"To hell with that," said the Marine. "I gotta get back to my outfit." He climbed painfully over the sea wall and disappeared into the never-never land of battle.

"There were a lot like him," Johnston observed later.

As the survivors of 1/8 came stumbling ashore, Shoup flung them piecemeal into the area Hawkins had just cleared.

"As soon as you can get enough men together," he told Major Hays, "I want you to push downbeach and see if you can't break through to Ryan."

Midmorning came and went, and Hays was still trying to build up a cohesive unit. Although his men were in contact with the enemy, he still lacked the strength to launch profitably any kind of assault into that dangerous and bristling stretch between Shoup's sector and Ryan's. Hawkins and his Scout-Snipers were still in good shape and ready to take on anything; Shoup now sent them into the airplane revetments beside the airstrip, where snipers had been causing havoc in Hays's staging area. In typical headlong Marine fashion, Hawkins' men rushed the revetments and killed several Japanese before they had time to react.

This minor success, coupled with Hawkins' earlier beach-clearing feat, enabled Colonel Presley Rixey to drag five sections of pack howitzers into a good shooting position. Two of these guns were maneuvered painstakingly until their field of fire included one of the twin Pocket strongpoints. Using a delayed-fuse setting, the gunners knocked it out and drove a few of the supporting automatic-weapons crews deeper underground. (This gun, along with its twin, had killed more Marines than any other weapon on Betio.) Rixey then turned his muzzles toward the lagoon, where the incessant rattle of gunfire from the *Saida Maru* could clearly be heard. After twelve successive hits on the freighter, it was obvious that the fire was ineffective, and it was canceled. The Navy boat-control officer (aboard the *Monrovia*) held up Major Hays's fifth and final wave so that a flight of carrier planes could dive-bomb the hulk. Colonel Shoup watched scornfully as they zoomed down one after another, dropping bombs that for the most part splashed harmlessly in the water. Shoup decided it was time to send a force of dynamite-toting engineers to clear out the ship.

After a wary approach from the blind side, Sergeant Willard Crossfield and his group (from 18th Marines) reached the barnacled hull and paused there for a few minutes. Two Nambu guns were chattering away in short bursts on the other side, the echoes rolling around inside the hold. Crossfield and his group now worked their way forward under the prow bulge, slipping over to the shore side of the ship. After scouting the partially submerged main deck and finding no one, Crossfield climbed to the third deck and, peering over the lip, saw several men, some chatting and puffing cigarettes, some stretched out, the rest busy with the guns. Back with his radioman in hip-deep water a few minutes later, Crossfield contacted Colonel Shoup and described what he had seen. Shoup, judging that the patrol lacked the strength to take on a force of that size with certain success, ordered him back to the beach; he was going to have to try something else.

After the patrol had reported in, Shoup called down the heavy naval gunfire he had been hoping to avoid. With the hulk lying so close to shore, it was a delicate gunnery problem; an overshot could easily land among the Marines on the island. But there were no mishaps, and by the time the battleships *Maryland* and *Colorado* had finished their thunderous fire mission, the old Japanese freighter was little more than a smoking mass of twisted steel.

4

THE
TURNING POINT

Oonuki was still alive; but he had little opportunity to rejoice over his survival. Something heavy was weighing him down with claustrophobic pressure. He called softly for help. There was no answer. He reached out with his free arm and grabbed hold of the first object offering purchase. He yanked—and came away with a greasy handful of cooked flesh.

Gradually Oonuki managed to work his way clear, and he sat for a long time listening to the scattered sounds of firing. Occasionally he could hear men talking in English. When at last he dared to peek through the hole, what he saw was a chaotic and awesome panorama of destruction, dotted with the coral-dusted corpses of his countrymen. The water of the lagoon was not quite visible from his vantage, but he could make out the superstructure of an American ship of some size, probably one of the destroyers. He crawled back among the charred bodies and tried to relax. He had no plans, nor any impulse to form any. He would merely wait. For what, he did not know.

Colonel Shoup was talking with someone over the phone, and Sherrod heard him say:

"We're in a mighty tough spot."

He noticed that the officer's hands trembled every so often; Shoup had been under strain now for many hours on end. What Sherrod did not know was that the colonel's leg wounds were beginning to hurt him rather badly. Seeing the correspondent sitting there, Shoup limped over and told him he had just got word that the Sixth Marines were not far out to sea, and closing fast. That was good news, to be sure, but Shoup was still worried. When J. C. Smith asked him at about this time if he thought he had enough men, his answer included this comment:

Situation ashore doesn't look good.

Close to noon the edge of the surf began lapping around the boondockers of the men in the beach working parties. Too late to be of help to anyone, the laggard tide was finally creeping in. The reef that had been such a catastrophic obstacle for the Higgins boats was soon awash with water that could have floated them right up to the sea wall.

It had taken Lawrence Hays more than five hours to get his battalion ashore. When it was done, around noon, he found that of the eight-hundred-odd men he started out with, nearly three hundred and fifty had been hit while trying to cross the reef. There was some profit to it all, though, for more than four hundred able-bodied Marines had been made available for the push inland; and it was this extra increment of power— bedraggled though it was—that enabled Colonel Shoup to get something rolling at long last.

Before one o'clock the tempo of the battle picked up considerably as groups of riflemen and demolition teams began leapfrogging across the main runway. After Colonel Walter Jordan had watched several of his fire teams race past the wrecked Zeroes and disappear in the garbage-dumplike landscape on the far side, he sent a runner across to find out how far their attack had carried them and what their condition was. The runner never reported back. A second man was sent and he also vanished. Jordan called Colonel Shoup for advice, and Shoup issued one of his typically succinct orders.

Move your command post to the other side of the island, and report to me when you have control.

Around three o'clock Lieutenant Commander MacPherson, buzzing the ocean shore in his float plane, spotted some troops along the beach. At first he was unable to tell whether they were friend or foe, but on his second pass the men waved up at him and he saw teeth flashing in sunburned faces. Later he scribbled in his log: "There is no mistaking the smile of a grinning Marine."

It had taken Jordan two hours to locate the remnants of his rifle companies. Most of them, it turned out, were coiled up in an abandoned Japanese trench system near the south beach. There was sadly little of his battalion left: Captain Maxie Williams of Baker Company had sixty men; Captain Clanahan of Charlie had seventy-five; Captain Tynes of Easy, fifteen. Of Fox Company a scant nine remained. Everyone was low on ammunition, and there was no water at all. But these few men had done a great thing: they had cut the island in two, isolating one half of the Japanese garrison from the other half.

As Jordan's men battled their way across the center of the island, Major Michael Ryan was completing the conquest of Green Beach. Ryan had a little help from Providence, or so he would always believe. As he was briefing his company commanders for the attack, a slender, collegiate-looking Navy officer emerged from out of the debris, carrying a big TBX radio on his back.

"I'm Lieutenant Thomas Greene," he told the startled Marine officers. "Can you gentlemen use my services?"

"Does that thing work?" asked Ryan, eying the radio.

Greene obligingly twisted a dial, and the soft waterfall sound of static issued forth. Lieutenant Greene had both the authority and the means to call in heavy shellfire from one of the destroyers in the lagoon. Ryan now had all the support he needed. The Navy lieutenant was put to work at once, and soon a succession of five-inch shells were slamming into the wasteland, forcing the enemy to burrow even deeper. With the echo of the last salvo still reverberating out to sea, Ryan blew a blast on his whistle that sent his troops into the assault.

It was a little past 12:30 p.m., on the second day of battle, when they topped a small rise and found themselves overlooking the Pacific surf. They dug in, marveling at the ease with which they had taken the island's southwest corner. Ryan knew it would have been a different story without the slim Navy lieutenant and his radio.

When the news of Ryan's success reached the *Maryland*, there was high exultation on the bridge, and Smith lost no time relaying the news to Colonel Shoup. Now that Green Beach was in Marine hands, the Sixth regiment should be able to make its landing there with little trouble (up until this moment Smith had not known where he was going to land them). The general now ordered Colonel Holmes to put one of the three battalions ashore on Green and move inland as far as the airfield. Holmes picked 1st Battalion (1/6), which he considered the sharpest of the three, and got them ready to make a landing at dusk.

5

THE BRAVE AND THE NOT-SO-BRAVE

Watching the Scout-Snipers butcher their way through the ruins, Robert Sherrod had noticed how incongruously *casual* everyone seemed to have become. None of the attacks were performed in the manner of grand sweeping charges; rather there was a strange matter-of-factness about them that seemed almost leisurely. (Hundreds of feet of film were taken of this phase of the battle, and today you can see Marines strolling with apparent aimlessness during the battle for Betio, firing their rifles occasionally or lobbing grenades; sometimes a Marine will fall, but even that seems casual.) These men had been shot at so many times in the past few hours that, in a crazy kind of way, they had grown accustomed to it.

Sherrod was sitting against the side of an uncompleted barracks near Shoup's command post, when a bullet ricocheted off the structure and hit the leg of a Marine sitting beside him.

"I'm sure glad it was spent," the man said, casually picking up the .303-caliber slug. Sherrod reached out for it, and the Marine dropped it in his palm; it was hot, and Sherrod flicked it away abruptly, the Marines guffawing. The sniper kept firing at them—for their cover was inadequate—and Sherrod suddenly realized that getting shot at was no longer a novelty to him either. He shifted position, wriggling about tortuously until every part of his body was out of the sniper's line of fire.

Later he watched a young, dirty-faced private with the arresting name of Adrian Strange limp heavily back to the command post and demand a pack of cigarettes; he and his machine-gun crew had run out, he explained. Someone tossed him a pack of Camels and he lit up. He seemed quite unintimidated by the snipers roundabout; nor did the Marine brass sitting nearby impress him particularly. After his first drag, he turned garrulous.

"Well, I just got me a sniper," he bragged. "That's six today, and me a cripple!" He took another puff and blew smoke grandly. "Busted my ankle stepping in a hole yesterday."

At that moment a flurry of bullets buzzed overhead like angry hornets, and the begrimed Marine sneered loudly, "Shoot me down, ya son of a bitches!" He had not even bothered to duck. After finishing his smoke he limped back into the battle. None of the officers sitting there had tried to stifle the lad's swagger, or chide him for the insolent way he had demanded the cigarettes: everyone knew that it was the Adrian Stranges of the division who were conquering the enemy.

Not every Marine on Betio was bellicose and uncowed like Private Strange. Sherrod was present when Major John Schoettel stumbled up to the command post, looking flustered and wretched. Sherrod was surprised to note that the officer was on the verge of tears—Marines being ordinarily a carefully emotionless lot. Earlier that day Colonel Shoup had collected a few stragglers and turned them over to him, with orders to join in the general struggle to expand the Red 2 perimeter.

"What's the problem?" asked Shoup.

"Colonel, my men can't advance."

"They can't?" Shoup stared at the distraught officer. "Why not?"

Schoettel muttered and shuffled about, until Shoup finally dragged it out of him that a single machine gun was blocking the way.

Shoup did not bother to hide his disgust. "God Almighty," he said, spitting on the sand. "One machine gun!"

He had nothing to add to that. The shaky major turned and went back to the battle, his shoulders slumped.

He was gone hardly a minute when a loud report clapped close at hand and one of Shoup's bodyguards, Corporal Leonce Olivier, yelped in pain and clutched his leg. The trapped Japanese had finally succeeded in punching a hole through the wall of the air-raid shelter, and one of them had just fired his rifle through it. The colonel, already irritable because of his throbbing leg wounds and lack of sleep, became enraged.

"Hooper!"

"Sir?"

"Get those Japs out of there!"

There was no way into the shelter except through a narrow opening behind some baffles. The first part of the job was easy: Gunnery Sergeant Jared Hooper shoved several grenades inside, blasting the interior. The second part was hard. Hooper knew that the longhouse was probably compartmented and that the grenades had only scoured the vestibule. Yanking some debris from the entrance, he and another man rushed in, firing, and darted from one compartment to the next, and when it was over the Japanese inside were dead.

Lieutenant William Deane Hawkins had killed more Japanese than anyone on Betio, but he had also taken more chances.

"Aw, they can't hit me," someone heard him say. "They couldn't hit me with a shotgun at point-blank range." His disdain was unwarranted; he had already been wounded once. At around two o'clock that afternoon he showed up at Shoup's command post for the last time.

"They won't fight, Colonel," he said, throwing down his helmet in disgust. "The bastards won't fight."

In this he was referring to the timidity displayed by a few Marine fire teams he had just observed. Shoup immediately ordered him to take his Scout-Snipers and attack a series of compounds along the beach, off in the direction of the so-called Pocket. Without acknowledging that he had heard, Hawkins scooped up his helmet and sauntered away. Shoup saw that he was heading alone and unprotected into Japanese-held territory; he cupped his hands and yelled after him. Hawkins neither stopped nor turned around, but kept on walking toward a sand-covered bunker which Kyle's squads had been unable to "reduce" after repeated tries. Miraculously, Hawkins managed to complete his mad seventy-five-yard walk and flip a grenade through the aperture, ducking before the mound erupted in a geyser of sand. It was the kind of performance that brought you either a Medal of Honor or death, or both. It occurred to Shoup now that his swift young hero would probably not survive the day, let alone the battle.

During the downbeach attacks that followed, an incoming mortar round killed three of Hawkins' men and wounded him in the hand. He pushed the corpsman away.

"I came here to kill Japs," he said, "not to be evacuated."

Sergeant Morris Owens saw Hawkins make his final charge. "We were attacking a sort of fort at the base of a sandy knoll," said Owens, "and Hawk started tossing grenades from close up. He had got rid of maybe half a dozen when a heavy machine gun opened up and an explosive shell hit him in the shoulder. The blood just gushed out of him."

Gunnery Sergeant Hooper and three others carried the dying officer to Dr. Brukardt's hospital. The indefatigable surgeon, still on his feet without a break, went to work on him at once, for he was losing blood at an alarming rate; but it was too late.

That night William Hawkins lay out under the slowly wheeling Southern Cross, suspended in a morphine haze. He died before dawn. Thus ended the short career of an authentic foursquare Medal of Honor hero, a strange fierce fellow, younger than his years (thirty), whose greatest joy was to close with the enemy.

The embarrassingly wretched Major Schoettel was back again.

"Colonel, there are a thousand Marines back there on the beach," he whined, "and not one of them will follow me across the airfield!"

Shoup took the cold cigar out of his mouth and, as patiently as he could, gave him a lesson in leadership. "You've got to say, 'Who'll follow me?' If only ten follow you—well, that's the best you can do. But it's better than nothing."

Once again the disgraced and humiliated officer turned and went back.

Colonel Walter Jordan had little sympathy for the man. "Like all combat troops, there are always a few yellow bellies in the Marines," he said later. "In any battle you'll find the fighting men up front. Then you'll find others who will linger behind, or find some excuse to come back to the rear. It has always been that way and always will be. The hell of it is, in any battle you lose a high percentage of your best men."

David Shoup recalled Schoettel a bit more compassionately. "While this officer, whatever the odds against him, perhaps ought to have been court-martialed, you really don't gain anything by that in the long run. He had lost all his men, or thought he had, and that shook him up pretty bad."[1]

[1] Major John Schoettel redeemed his honor in subsequent campaigns, was cited for bravery, and died with his boots on. Transferred to the 22nd Marines after Tarawa, he served as shore party commander at Eniwetok, where he was recommended for the Bronze Star. Following the Marshalls campaign, he was given command of another rifle battalion (2/22) and took part in the capture of Guam. During that action he was wounded but later returned to duty. He was killed on August 16th, 1944, near the end of the operation.

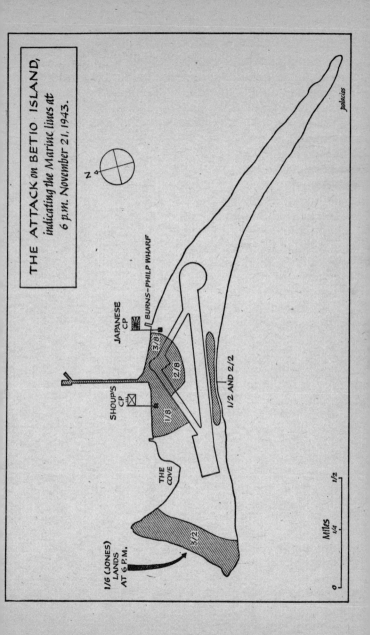

THE ATTACK on BETIO ISLAND, indicating the Marine lines at 6 p.m. November 21, 1943.

1/6 (JONES) LANDS AT 6 P.M.

THE COVE

3/2

SHOUP'S CP

1/8

2/8

3/8

JAPANESE CP

BURNS–PHILP WHARF

1/2 AND 2/2

palacios

N

Miles

0   1/4   1/2

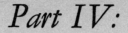

Part IV:

THE
VICTORY

1.

"... WE ARE WINNING"

Reports were coming in from all units that the Japanese were beginning to kill themselves in appreciable numbers.

It is written in the *Senjikun* battle ethics, "I will never suffer the disgrace of being taken alive." And so the surviving individuals of the Betio garrison were methodically blowing themselves up, shooting themselves, disemboweling themselves—choosing suicide as a last desperate means of avoiding that disgrace. The advancing Marines stumbled across Japanese sailors who had thrust bayonets into their own bellies, and grenade-suicides with missing hands and bloody nubs where their heads used to be. Other men shot themselves in the mouth, pushing the triggers of their Arisakas with their big toes. In one dugout alone the Marines found seventeen men, every one a suicide.

Shoup knew it was only a question of time now. At 4 p.m. he remarked to Sherrod, "Well, I think we're winning—but the bastards have a lot of bullets left." He then sat down against the rear wall of the air-raid shelter and scratched out a laconic message to General Julian Smith, a message that told the general the darkest hour of the battle was past.

Casualties: many. Percentage dead: not known. Combat efficiency: we are winning.

The general immediately relayed the message intact to Holland Smith up at Makin, and "Howlin' Mad" is said to have smiled at Kelly Turner for the first time in weeks.

Julian Smith received word from MacPherson at about this time that he had spotted groups of Japanese wading across the partially submerged, two-mile-long sandspit that stretched from the tail of Betio to the neighboring island of Bairiki. In response the general ordered the Sixth Marines' Colonel Holmes to put another of his three landing teams ashore there—

. . . to prevent withdrawal of hostile forces to the east.

Holmes picked Lieutenant Colonel Raymond Murray's 2nd Battalion, Sixth. Murray and his men had been ready to follow Major William K. Jones's 1st Battalion onto Green Beach, and were disappointed to a man to learn that they were being sent instead to clean up the minor garbage of the great battle. At around 4:30 p.m. carrier planes began dive-bombing and strafing Bairiki in preparation for the landing. Targets were almost non-existent; the only visible fortification stood at the eastern tip, facing Betio—a lone pillbox. Inside it were fifteen Japanese who for reasons unknown had dragged a drum of aviation gasoline in with them. One of the Hellcats' fifty-caliber bullets passed through the gunport and, with a puff of flame and black smoke, all potential resistance to Murray's landing was "neutralized." By five o'clock the battalion was safely ashore and in position to block all would-be fugitives. What no one realized yet was that some two hundred Japanese, many of them armed, were already on their way up the twenty-five-mile-long chain of islands beyond Bairiki. Murray and his men were soon to follow them, and would get a taste of the action they craved.

*   *   *

Major Henry Crowe had watched the bombing and strafing. "Look at those planes," he scoffed. "They haven't killed a Jap in two days."

Crowe was already in a sour mood; the best he had been able to do this second day was to strengthen his position and get ready for tomorrow when, hopefully, his battalion would be able to break out of its constricted perimeter. Crowe had thrown several assaults against the Burns-Philp wharf, but all he had to show for it was a casualty-riddled Fox Company. The most formidable position blocking his way was a large blockhouse or bombproof shelter, the biggest on Betio, that squatted hugely over the center of his line. He had sent Lieutenant Alexander Bonnyman and his engineers up against it, but they had been driven back time after time. Crowe's men had killed scores of Japanese but—as he was overheard complaining to Colonel Shoup—no matter how many they killed, it seemed that more always came filtering up from the tail of the island.

"Where in hell are they all coming from?" he wanted to know. "Do they have a tunnel to Tokyo or something?"

Late in the day he called in naval gunfire on the big blockhouse; a destroyer, answering the call, ran in so close to shore that it seemed in danger of scraping the bottom of the lagoon. Flames spouted from the five-inch guns; a moment later came an answering crash as the rounds landed. Altogether some eighty shells pounded the area around the building, winking like giant flashbulbs.

"They never hit it squarely," said Crowe glumly when it was over. "Just almost."

Crowe and his men had no way of knowing that the building in question was the headquarters of the Betio garrison, or that inside the honeycombed fortress a Japanese admiral was waiting calmly for the end. The move that Shibasaki had contemplated (shifting his flag to a secondary headquarters near the ocean shore) had proved impossible; he was trapped where he was. As sunset approached, the boyish-looking admiral composed what was to be his final message to Tokyo.

> Our weapons have been destroyed. From now on everyone is attempting a final charge. May Japan exist for ten thousand years!

William Jones and his men (1/6) now became the first battalion to reach Betio without getting shot to pieces in the water; their unopposed landing on Green Beach was completed after dark. Michael Ryan's dirty, ragged, dead-tired remnant greeted the reinforcements with joy and relief. These tough fighters had been isolated for two days, waging their own semi-private battle to stay alive while they slaughtered the enemy. Now, as the fresh, heavily armed columns filtered smartly through their lines and dug in for the night, Ryan and his survivors knew that they were going to live to see a better day.

Julian Smith decided that it was high time his man ashore got some rest; Shoup had been at it now for some thirty hours. After a final conference aboard the *Maryland,* Colonel Merritt Edson came ashore with orders to bring the battle to a close as soon as possible. A submarine had been reported a few miles to the northeast; for all anyone knew, there could be several submarines on the way, and Admiral Hill wanted to get his ships out of the area. Edson arrived at the command post at around 8:30 p.m., informing Shoup that, while the general thought he had done a satisfactory job, it was time for him to step down.

David Shoup's feelings at this moment were decidedly ambivalent. He knew that he was no longer as sharp as he might be, and sorely needed the relief; yet he regretted having to give the reins over to another just when the battle was entering its final phase. But he said nothing and took Edson into the longhouse where, amid the putrefying corpses, they studied the maps by flashlight and worked out a battle plan for the third day.

Afterward, Shoup had his leg wounds redressed, swallowed a couple of aspirin, and stretched out on the sand in a spot where he hoped no one would step on him. The whole thing was now Merritt Edson's headache.

Petty Officer Oonuki had kept himself hidden in the smashed hospital dugout most of that second day. Late in the afternoon he decided to try and escape to Bairiki. It seemed a good time to go, for there were no battle sounds coming from the tapering tail of the island. As soon as it got dark he stripped and buried his clothes in the sand floor of the dugout (afterward he was at a loss to explain why). Venturing outside, he found that he was in worse shape than he had thought; he could hardly take a step without staggering. Carefully he made his way through the shattered trees and bushes straight down the tail. During this perilous trek he glimpsed many shifting, darting shadows and was fired on twice. At land's end he stepped into the cool surf and began wading. The water never got any deeper than three or four feet. Halfway across, he made out a figure some distance ahead of him, moving in the same direction—but he made no effort to catch up.

About an hour after moonrise, he stepped onto the Bairiki beach and was immediately confronted with the ruins of the Hellcat-destroyed bunker. Oonuki blundered right inside, looking for food and water, unprepared for the sight that greeted him by moonlight through the gunport. He had naïvely thought of Bairiki as a kind of haven, where he would be able to link up with the holdouts he figured were congregating there, waiting for reinforcements from Truk or the Marshalls —sure to arrive soon. When he saw the tangle of charred bodies, looking so much like those he had left behind in the bunker on Betio, it all seemed suddenly too much. A crushing wave of despair took hold and overwhelmed him; the only thing he could think of was suicide. He reached down and felt around for something to cut his wrists with. There was nothing but a seashell. He began scraping himself with it as hard as he could; but he was too weak, and found it impossible to force the blunt edge through his skin. Giving that up eventually, he sank down and cried himself to sleep.

2

MAKIN AGAIN

Holland Smith was, as we have seen, thoroughly disgusted by the tentative and timid performance of Ralph Smith's Army troops on Makin Atoll. He thought they should have secured the weakly defended island of Butaritari by nightfall, D-day. "Any Marine regiment would have done it in that time," he said later, pointing out that the 22nd Marines captured Engebi, a far stronger target, in seven hours. Nor had Smith forgotten his last experience with Army troops—when overcautious GIs required more than two weeks to capture Attu in the Aleutians.

By noon H. M. Smith was really howling mad. Unable to keep his somewhat bulbous nose out of it any longer, he stormed ashore to see for himself exactly what the problem was. Almost immediately he ran into an Army infantry company whose men were firing so indiscriminately that a working party in the area had had to take cover. Smith confronted the company commander.

"What the hell are you firing at?"

"I'm trying to clean out the snipers in the area, sir."

"Can't you see there aren't any Japs around here?"

The officer mumbled that he was only following orders.

"If I hear one more shot from your men," warned Smith, "I'll take your damn weapons away from you!"

At Ralph Smith's command post he was told there was "heavy fighting" at the northern end of Butaritari, delaying final capture of the island. The Marine general took a jeep and drove to the scene of the reported action. It was, in his words, "as quiet as Wall Street on Sunday."

Returning to Ralph Smith's headquarters, he ordered the Army general to go and take a look at what his officers called heavy fighting.

That night turned out to be one of the most exasperating nights of Holland Smith's life. "I slept under a mosquito net on a cot set outside the tent. I hoped the presence of Ralph Smith and myself would be a good influence on the sentries posted around the camp. I was mistaken." Shots snapped back and forth over his head throughout the night, drilling holes in the tent and actually clipping coconuts off the trees. Smith was sure there were no Japanese within a mile of the place. He yearned to be with his fire-disciplined Marines on Tarawa.

The ships at sea had one minor brush with the Imperial Navy. Admiral Harry Hill had read an intelligence analysis on the second day indicating that the enemy was trying to mass submarine strength in the waters west of Tarawa; the first subs were expected to arrive in the area on November 23rd. One showed up before that. At noon the destroyer *Gansevoort* reported sonar contact a few thousand yards from the transport area. An hour later *Meade* reported sonar contact. Both destroyers cruised around the area, making contact from time to time. Not until five o'clock did the sonar pings become definitive enough to justify an attack. *Meade* and *Frazier* took turns depth-charging the zone where the enemy sub was believed to be, and at 5:30 p.m. a periscope was sighted between the two destroyers; moments later the gray spine of Imperial Navy submarine *I-35* broke the surface. Crews from both destroyers crowded the railings to gawk; the sub lay close broadside to *Frazier.* That ship's commanding officer, Lieutenant Commander Elliott Brown, now decided that the thing to do was to ram. The turn was made and the

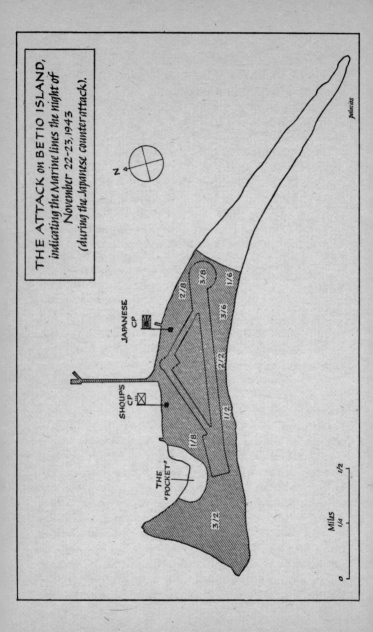

THE ATTACK on BETIO ISLAND,
indicating the Marine lines the night of
November 22-23, 1943
(during the Japanese counterattack).

N

JAPANESE CP

SHOUP'S CP

THE "POCKET"

2/8
3/8
1/6
3/6
2/2
1/2
1/8
3/2

Miles

0   1/4   1/2

paleries

I-35 was battered with a great crunch just abaft of the conning tower. As the *Frazier* backed away, several Japanese crewmen erupted out of the tower hatch—not intending to abandon ship, as those at the railings assumed, but to man the deck gun. *Frazier* loomed so close alongside that her sailors were able to prevent this by pistol fire. *I-35* began to settle in the water and then, abruptly, she plunged headfirst into the Pacific depths. The destroyers launched whaleboats to pick up four swimming survivors, members of the deck-gun crew, one of whom whipped out a pistol and started shooting as his would-be rescuers drew near; he was submachine-gunned to death.

Finally, in a typical, slightly ludicrous *Galvanic* contretemps, one of the returning whaleboats was mistaken for a sub by a patrolling U. S. Navy plane—and bombed; the sailors were only shaken up, however, by the 500-pounder that exploded beside them. The plane itself was then fired at by *Meade*'s anti-aircraft gunners and two hits were scored. The pilot managed to steer his wobbly Grumman back to the carrier, none the worse for wear but perhaps somewhat wiser.

3

BETIO

Overrunning the Enemy Headquarters

From here on it was a businesslike affair and, from a tactical standpoint, rather uninteresting—but no less bloody than the first two days had been. The difference was that it was almost exclusively Japanese blood that was spilled now.

William Jones launched his attack down the Betio bird's back (the south shore) at 8:15 on the third morning. With three tanks—including the indestructible "China Gal"—fifty yards in the lead, Charlie Company spearheaded the push with a line that was only a hundred yards wide. The other two companies followed in broader formation, mopping up. As usual the enemy was rarely to be seen. Occasionally a Marine would glimpse a small figure bobbing along in the distance, but generally the Japanese were visible—if they were visible at all—in the form of corpses. (The Betio garrison conducted its ferocious defense almost entirely from underground positions, peering through tiny firing holes.)

Charlie Company reached Walter Jordan's south beach enclave at around eleven o'clock, after killing some two hundred and fifty Japanese in an eight-hundred-yard thrust. With this link-up, roughly half the island was in Marine hands—everything west of the pier except the Pocket.

"We've got 'em by the balls now!" said Major Culhane, the regimental operations officer, and most everyone at the command post agreed that things were looking good.

Colonel Holmes's one remaining battalion, 3/6 (Lieutenant Colonel Kenneth McLeod), now landed on Green around noon and raced down the southern shore, retracing the path carved out that morning. Coming up to the rear of Major Jones's positions, McLeod had his men dig in along a secondary or backup line, ready to provide support for 1/6 if need be.

The need would in fact arise that very evening, when the Japanese launched their long-delayed counterattack.

In the indecisive fighting on the second day it had become clear to Crowe that there were three distinct positions holding his battalion in check. Expanding his share of the beachhead would be impossible until these three were knocked out of the way. The most formidable was Shibasaki's bombproof. The second was a steel pillbox just inland from the Burns-Philp wharf. The third was an ordinary coconut-log emplacement directly in front of the bombproof. The three positions were mutually supporting, meaning that it was impossible to attack one without coming under fire from the other two. Crowe lost more than a little sleep trying to conceive a plan of attack that would not cost him half of his already depleted battalion.

The action began at 9:30 a.m. the third morning. Crowe prefaced the infantry attack with a mortar barrage on the log emplacement. At the same time Lieutenant Largey in "Colorado" pumped a series of 75-mm. shells at the steel cupola over on the left. Under this covering fire, the men of King and Fox companies got to their feet and moved forward cautiously. As the enemy counterfire began building up to an intimidating pitch, fortune intervened on the side of the attackers. One

81-mm. mortar round penetrated the log emplacement's ammunition dump, and the entire position went up in multiple
geysers of flame and sand and wood. There was more. Even
before the last echo rolled away across the waters, Largey's
cannon had pried open a hole in the steel pillbox and followed
up with two more rounds that finished the men inside it.

Shibasaki's headquarters now lay open to direct assault.

Crowe quickly exploited the break by sending forward a
platoon from the 18th Marines, with Alexander Bonnyman
again in command. This blond, All-America-looking lieutenant
(a Princeton graduate who incidentally owned a silver mine
in New Mexico) crawled up the sandbagged western face of
the bombproof with five men, as others hosed down the crest
with a stream of bullets. Aided by flame throwers and demolitions, he made it all the way to the top, and for one dramatic moment the Marines held the island's highest ground.
Granted it was only seventeen feet above sea level—but to
Bonnyman it was a veritable eminence.

The Japanese, intent on saving their headquarters, counterattacked suddenly and with the usual suicidal abandon, and
Alexander Bonnyman was transformed in a twinkling from
an ordinary dutiful Marine into a Medal of Honor hero (post-
humous). It would have been simple enough to withdraw
down the slope, but something made him stand his ground,
blazing away with his carbine on full automatic as the Japanese came on. He was hit: dropping to his knees, he changed
magazines and delivered a final spray of snub-nosed bullets
into the men struggling up the sandy slope. When his half-
minute stand was over and the last of the counterattackers
had turned and fled, Bonnyman was seen to slump forward
and roll part of the way downhill, coming to rest against a
Japanese who, like the others in sight, lay dead (or dying)
around the base of the mound.

Bonnyman's engineers now scrambled upslope and dropped
grenades down the bombproof's air vents. After the first muffled explosions, clusters of frantic men began pouring out of

the east and south exits. The Marines threw themselves down behind their rifles, ready to beat off another counterattack; but the Japanese were only running for their lives, dodging through the weird blasted wasteland that stretched toward the tail of the island. Every Marine in the area fired into the dwindling mobs and a howitzer crew, with one devastating round of canister shot, slaughtered twenty-odd men in a shallow defile at the end of the airfield.

Crowe sent his cheering companies surging around both sides and on beyond the fallen bombproof—while a bulldozer was brought forward from the beach and immediately began to heap sand up against the exits, sealing the remaining Japanese inside. Other Marines poured jerry cans of gasoline down the air vents and dropped lighted matches in after; with a loud whoosh and a few echoing shrieks, the men inside were broiled and suffocated to death. More than a hundred and fifty died by this ghastly mop-up method, probably including Shibasaki himself (although his body was never found).

With their headquarters captured, the Japanese in that sector seemed en masse to lose their will to resist. As Crowe's jubilant Marines raced straight across the island, they came upon an estimated ninety enemy sailors who had obviously killed themselves only moments before.

By the end of the day Crowe had linked his force up with the Jones-Jordan line. The 2nd Marine Division now held nearly three-quarters of the island: everything but the tail and that four-acre patch overlooking the cove called the Pocket.

4

COUNTERATTACK
Prelude

Late that afternoon Sherrod, certain that the show was as good as over, hitched a ride out to the troopship *Virgo*. Some of the ship's crew, anxious for news of the battle, gathered around him as soon as he came aboard, and there were grins all around when he told them it wouldn't be long now. One sailor remarked, "I'd have given anything if I could have been over there to help out," and a junior-grade lieutenant said wistfully, "This is the first time I've had a chance to do anything"—as he loaned Sherrod his shaving gear. A Negro mess steward brought him a sandwich and a glass of iced tea. The ship's captain, Claton McLaughlin, insisted on turning his cabin over to the correspondent and even rounded up a typewriter for him to use. To Robert Sherrod, who had been existing in a world of sweat, gore and putrefaction for what seemed like a week at least, the *Virgo* was a veritable paradise of cleanliness and order. The weary *Time-Life* man peeled off his dirty dungarees and luxuriated for a while under a cool shower; all he wanted to do now was write up his articles and catch the first plane out, and leave bloody Tarawa far behind forever.

There was more news from shore, however—news that would drag him back to that stinking nightmare of an island, notebook in hand. For even as he sat down at the captain's desk and began to type, the first of three counterattacks began.

The tactical situation could not have been much simpler at this point in the battle. The Marines held the airfield and everything west of it except the Pocket; most of the Japanese survivors were trapped in the long tapering tail that made up the rest of the island. William Jones's three companies had taken over the line, from the ocean beach all the way across the island to the lagoon shore. Baker Company, under Lieutenant Norman Thomas (Long Beach, Miss.), was dug in on the oceanside flank; it was this hundred-man unit that was to bear the brunt of the Japanese attack. Thomas, a tight-lipped sobersides of a fellow (his men called him Hard Tom), had only taken over Baker Company six hours earlier, when the company commander was wounded.

As the swift tropical night came racing in from the east, silence settled over the battlefield, broken occasionally by the faint scuffing of shovels. The Marines on Jones's line sat in their holes and kept most of their attention on the bushes and trees across the way. At seven o'clock came the first sign of trouble: an eerie, high-pitched cry like that of some jungle beast. A loon laughed. Baboons screamed and cockatoos whistled; monkeys chattered, wolves howled—a continuous cacophony of weird sounds that were meant to frighten and intimidate. By now every Marine on the island knew that the long-delayed counterattack was about to begin. No one knew how many Japanese were still alive, and there was much nervous speculation on the probable size of the attacking force.

The Japanese about to hit the Marine line were more interested in self-sacrifice than anything else. It was a rare Japanese fighting man whose mind was not haunted by dreams of death; most of them believed that dying in battle was a consummation devoutly to be wished.

Corpses drifting swollen in the sea-depths,
Corpses rotting in the mountain-grass;
We shall die. By the side of the Emperor we shall die.
We shall not look back.
          —from a Japanese Army manual.

The most recent large-scale example of this peculiarly Japanese attitude had been the final charge on Attu, which ended the Aleutians campaign earlier that year. Colonel Shigei Yamazaki had recognized by May 28th that defeat was inevitable; the food was gone and there was little ammunition. His original force of twenty-six hundred had been cut down to a thousand by the Americans. Late in the afternoon he had called his men together at an old Russian sealing station, where he told them it was time to die. Only by self-sacrifice, he said (after killing as many Americans as possible), could they express the sincerity of their purpose to the enemy and at the same time fulfill their oaths as Warriors of Nippon. Yamazaki's thousand shouted that they were ready to die.

After the cold mists rolled in and the light of day faded, the sick and the wounded who were unable to participate in the last charge were killed—shot in the head or given fatal injections of barbiturates. Shortly after midnight the rest came creeping down from the barren hills, many armed only with knives and bayonets. In a furious *banzai* attack, they broke through the American picket line and overran a quartermaster depot and all but annihilated the staff and the patients of a field hospital. With a few exceptions, those Japanese not killed in the fighting committed suicide rather than let themselves be captured.

The Japanese on Betio, likewise defenders of a lost cause, sought their own glorious deaths and hoped to take a few Americans along.

Banzai!
Every man on the line heard it. The time was 7:30 p.m.
Marines, we come to drink your blood!

All at once fifty Japanese rose up out of the bushes and raced in a tight howling mob toward the junction of Able and Baker companies at the airfield turning-circle, appearing so suddenly that the Marines had time to cut down only a few as the rest broke through to the rear. Lieutenant Norman Thomas first became aware of the attack when he heard "a terrible screaming" and the sounds of men running his way. He said later it was so dark at this point that all he could see were the muzzle flashes of Marines' weapons reflected in Japanese officers' sabers; the enemy seemed to be flowing past his foxhole on both sides. It was a paralyzing situation—for a few moments anyway; finally he groped for the field phone, intending to call down howitzer fire in front of Baker Company, hoping to wipe out the sailors he figured rightly were massing there. Before he could utter a word, a Japanese with a bayoneted rifle loomed overhead and dropped into the hole with him. The two men grappled frantically—Thomas expecting to feel cold steel in his flesh every time they changed holds—with Thomas managing at last to unlimber his pistol and fire into the man's chest. The Japanese flopped heavily, and Thomas—taking no chances—put the muzzle against the man's temple and blew his head apart. His adrenalin racing now, Thomas reholstered the pistol, threw the gory corpse violently out of the hole, and sat back, panting. Once more he reached for the phone.

As for the rest of the attackers who had broken through the gap, they were put to death one by one as they pivoted madly here and there like so many impalas, looking for Marines to kill. It was relatively easy work, for the Japanese made no attempt to seek cover. The job was done by 8:30 p.m.

5

COUNTERATTACK
The Last Gasp

So certain were the Marines of a second attack that they left their wounded where they lay, reluctant to weaken the line by assigning men as stretcher-bearers.

William Jones's 1st Battalion, Sixth, had been in action since 8:15 that morning. The long advance down the southern shore and now the preliminary, probing, night attack had left the men with little energy to spare; officers were not surprised to hear the furtive sounds of snoring up and down the line. Sergeants were soon crawling from hole to hole, shaking the sleepers roughly, whispering dire warnings of what would happen if they fell under again.

The artillery that Lieutenant Thomas had called for now began landing in great island-shaking salvos, like freight trains out of the sky. Spotters on the line reported that the shells were landing from fifty to seventy-five yards in front of Baker Company's line—as close as anybody cared to have them. When the barrage lifted, the young officer picked up the phone again and contacted his battalion commander.

"Major Jones, we need reinforcements."

"Can't do it," was the reply. Jones had no men to send, and

it would have been impossibly difficult to bring up any of Crowe's men in the sniper-infested darkness. Thomas was on his own.

The second attack began at 11 o'clock with the Japanese stirring up a diversion in the Able Company sector, i.e., in the middle of the cross-island line. Enemy soldiers called out from the bushes and lobbed a few grenades, and the men of Able tensed for a full-scale attack; but there was only silence for ten minutes.

Once again the assault, when it came, was against Baker Company. Rows of enemy skirmishers stepped clear of the palm trees and advanced at a trot. That the assault was stopped and driven back was due in large part to the combative spirit of three Marine machine gunners.

Private Horace C. Warfield (Houston, Tex.) had seen the Number 1 gunner killed at the start of the attack, and jumped behind the weapon himself. He had got off a long burst into a group that was silhouetted in the glow of the smouldering fires, when a man leaped into his foxhole and thrust a bayonet through his thigh. Warfield wrapped his arms around the thrashing man and held onto him until another Marine, Pfc. Lowell Koci, brained him with the butt of his rifle. Without a thought for his copiously bleeding wound, Warfield resumed his place behind the machine gun. The platoon's Number 2 gunner was also killed in the first moments of the action. Pfc. James L. Edwards (Thayer, Mo.), taking his place, was immediately hit in the shoulder and arm, but ignored his wounds long enough to squeeze off a series of sweeping bursts into the oncoming figures. The story was essentially the same on the Number 3 gun except that the original gunner, Pfc. Daniel W. Ness (Black Hills, S.D.), was wounded, not killed. Like Warfield and Edwards, he ignored the pain and kept firing throughout the attack until the surviving Japanese faded away into the darkness. Of the three gunners, perhaps

James Edwards' courage and faithfulness to duty were the most impressive, for he believed his wounds to be fatal.

Nothing much happened for the next two hours, and the Marines began to wonder if it wasn't all over at last; but then the moon worked its way out of the haze on the horizon, and Jones's men could see by its light that the Japanese were assembling for still another attack, groups of them moving to and fro beyond the tree line. At three o'clock two machine guns opened up in front of Baker Company. Spotters reported to Lieutenant Thomas that the Nambus were emplaced in a couple of wrecked trucks thirty or so yards in front of 3rd Platoon's position. Their fire was harmless enough, but bothersome; it forced Marines' heads down when every man needed to stay alert for the imminent assault.

A lone Japanese bomber now put in an appearance, making two low passes over the island. It seemed as if the pilot was trying to get the Marines to reveal their positions so that he could bomb them; but he drew no fire at all. Finally he dropped an ineffectual cluster of fifty-pounders which exploded near the deserted airplane revetments, and headed out to sea.

At 4 a.m. on the fourth day of battle, with the moon raising grotesque shadows across the coral flats, some three hundred Japanese launched the Betio garrison's final effort. Men brandishing swords and long knives flowed abruptly into the Marine lines. The fighting that followed was savage and primitive, with almost everyone out of ammunition; many who died in the next few minutes were choked or clubbed to death.

Pfc. Jack Stambaugh, a lantern-jawed farm boy from Bowie, Texas, found himself in the very thick of it. First his rifle jammed; next he heard someone yelling for help in the adjoining hole. Stambaugh jumped up—but found his way blocked by a naked man, armed, as Stambaugh was, with a bayoneted rifle. The Marine executed a conventional "parry and thrust" and yanked his blade free, the man slumping to the sand. Three loinclothed men now approached him menacingly, one at a time, and Stambaugh engaged each in turn; soon there were four Japanese on the sand around him. The Marine who had called for help now yelled a warning, for someone was approaching Stambaugh on his blind side. Stambaugh whirled, but not fast enough, and a Japanese officer thrust him through with a saber. That was Jack Stambaugh's first and last fight. (The brief encounter, which lasted less than thirty seconds and left all participants dead, had been witnessed by a wounded private named Harold L. Carstens— the one who had yelled the warning. Because of his wounds and the unpredictable movement of the combatants he had been unable to intervene.)

The general melee did not last long, but at one point the surge of Japanese threatened to overwhelm the line, and Lieutenant Thomas found himself shouting into the field phone:

"We're killing them as fast as they come, but we can't hold much longer. We've got to have reinforcements."

Major Jones shouted back: "You've got to hold!"

Hold they did, and by five o'clock the *banzai* attack had run its course and some two hundred Japanese lay lifeless within the Marine lines, with a hundred more out front where the artillery had come crashing down during the fight.

"I guess that's it," said Thomas into the phone, somewhat calmer now. "Can you send up stretcher-bearers?"

Waiting for those stretcher-bearers, he was amazed to hear a couple of roosters crowing from the tail of the island, raucously heralding the dawn of a new day.

Later Norman Thomas walked back to the battalion command post and gave Major Jones a laconic verbal report on the events of the most exciting night of his life. Then he went over to the trenchlike tank trap where the wounded lay, and talked quietly with a few of his men. Still later, just after dawn, a Marine correspondent found him propped up against a tree, staring glazedly at the carpet of contorted bodies that lay before him, stretching off toward the tip of the island. The correspondent asked if he would mind answering a few questions, and Thomas said he wouldn't mind. His eyes were bleary with fatigue, and he spoke so softly that the correspondent had to lean close to hear.

"They really stood up to it, didn't they?" He shook his head in wonder, proud of the way his men had held their ground. "Every damn one of them a champion," he added. With that, "Hard Tom" dropped off into a heavy slumber, and the correspondent closed his notebook.[1]

* * *

The three counterattacks, not overly impressive to anyone except Thomas and company, were futile minor efforts—delaying actions in which lives were exchanged for time that had no military value at all. They were not the calculated forays of men holding out in expectation of relief; the Japanese garrison knew very well by now that no relief could possibly reach them in time. The only thing the holdouts hoped to gain—other than a niche at Yasakuni—was to keep one battered, smoking, useless atoll technically within the Greater East Asia Co-prosperity Sphere for a few hours longer.

[1] Lieutenant Norman Thomas was killed on Saipan a few months later.

6

IS IT OVER?

Later that morning Lieutenant Colonel Kenneth McLeod's untried 3rd Battalion, Sixth, moved up into line, relieving 1/6. Jones's men stumbled back to the rear and stretched out on the sand or sat in small groups, too tense to sleep, while McLeod and his fresh, eager-to-kill troops jumped off at 8 a.m.—with the invincible "Colorado" and "China Gal" leading the way. What followed was more slaughter than battle, for the enemy sailors were stunned and dazed and incapable of serious resistance. Yet only a handful surrendered, or were allowed to.

Uninhibited by the realization that the battle was nearly over and that life was sweet, it took the men of 3/6 only four and a half hours to reach the tip of the tail and, although it is not mentioned in the official record, the last few sorry stragglers were shot down at leisure as they tried to wade across to Bairiki. Thus the Sixth Marines had played the classical role of fresh reserves thrown in at the crucial pivot point of a battle. The two battalions which landed on Green Beach had provided the knockout punch for which the previous troops had set the enemy up, but were too groggy to deliver on their own.

Resistance in the Pocket was beginning to crumble, position by position. All the correspondents and combat photographers had gathered to watch the finale—and a grueling, grinding affair it was, involving a flanking maneuver from the reef and a succession of flame-thrower assaults that pulled the drawstring tighter and tighter.

Around noon a Hellcat piloted by Ensign W. W. Kelly (Castlewood, Pa.) buzzed low over the island, circled once, and landed on the airstrip, fishtailing around the Seabee bulldozers that were already at work. Kelly climbed down and shook hands with the Marines who came running up to him.

"Is it over?" he wanted to know.

They told him it was pretty nearly over. The begrimed men eyed him admiringly, for he was shaven and fresh-looking and made them yearn for the distant ships where there was hot food and cold showers, along with clean air to breathe. (The Betio air was by now so humid with the stench of rotting flesh that men paused casually to vomit, as if it was a routine function.) Kelly did not comment on the pervasive stink but he did mention the dead men he had seen floating several miles out to sea; there were a great many. He referred to them as Japs and some of them were; but eighty-eight Marines were missing—and remain missing to this day. Most of them had been carried away by the tide.

Early in the afternoon Julian Smith came ashore and, after a brief inspection and a conference with Edson, sent the following message to Admiral Hill:

> *Decisive defeat heavy enemy counterattack last night destroyed bulk of enemy resistance. Expect complete annihilation of enemy on Betio this date. . . .*

At 1:05 p.m. word came through that the Pocket had been completely overrun. Not a single prisoner had been taken in this action. At almost the same moment—just past one o'clock—a Marine from McLeod's battalion stepped into the gentle surf that lapped the easternmost end of Betio, the tip of the tail, and stooped down to splash his sweaty face with sea water. There were simply no more Japanese left to kill. It was all over. Smith relayed the news by field phone to all infantry units and by radio to the ships: the battle of Betio had come to an end—after seventy-six hours of the bitterest fighting in the history of the Corps. More than one thousand United States Marines lay dead in the sun, either stretched out on the coral or floating in the water somewhere.

That very hour, in a kind of anticlimax, Army General Ralph Smith flashed word to Admiral Turner:

Makin taken.

The sixty-five hundred soldiers of the hapless Army regiment had required three and a half days to capture an island whose garrison they outnumbered at least eight to one.[1] Army losses were light (64 dead, 150 wounded), but the U. S. *Navy* had paid dearly for Makin—as we shall see a little later.

Radio Tokyo was broadcasting its own version of the battle for the Gilberts; it made interesting listening for Turner's monitors. Tokyo was claiming that five thousand United States Marines had gone to the bottom in the sinking of three transports; that subsequently the Combined Fleet destroyed three carriers and shot down eighty-nine planes; that heavy fighting was still raging on Betio's beaches. Imperial headquarters then issued a separate bulletin which paid solemn tribute to those men—now in fact dead—whom they called "the flowers of the Pacific," and urged all soldiers, sailors and airmen of Japan to consider the magnificent deeds of the great warriors of Tarawa.

[1] Ralph Smith and his 27th Infantry Division never did have a successful campaign together; they performed poorly in the subsequent Marshalls operation, and on Saipan Holland M. Smith removed the luckless general from command for his failure to keep his troops apace with the Marine divisions on either flank.

7

THE CORPSES

David Shoup had been waiting impatiently for the enemy to fold. In the pocket of his dungaree jacket was a celluloid-wrapped card that would add to the Shoup legend: a sort of all-purpose surrender document, completely filled out except for signatures and designations of the units to be surrendered, it was valid for turning over anything from a squad right up to the Empire itself, practically. ("There was some question in my mind as to how you ended a battle," he explained later, "so I went to a library and studied up on it.") He never did accept the surrender, however—nor did anyone else, for there was none. In this all-or-nothing battle, only one Japanese officer remained alive out of the original garrison—a lieutenant, who had been away on a wood-gathering expedition and was captured later.

There remains but one final glimpse of Shoup on Betio. On the afternoon of the fourth day he found time to write a poem, in memory of a battalion commander he had admired.

> *Drag from my sight this*
> > *blear-eyed*
> *Thing*
> > *That was my friend.*
> *Return all to Mother Earth*

> *Except*
> *That ring*
> *To prove his end*
> *On Tarawa.*[1]

* * *

Some five thousand corpses lay putrefying under the merciless equatorial sun. Marines who had spent the last two days killing Japanese now found themselves collecting their victims into great piles—to be taken eventually out to sea in Higgins boats and unceremoniously dumped overboard. More care was taken with the dead Marines, needless to say, most of whom had been brought to a collection point near the base of the long pier—too many, it seemed, for at 3:50 that afternoon Merritt Edson received a somber message from Shore Party Control:

> *Request detail to clear the bodies around pier. Hindering shore party operation.*

A rough cemetery had been laid out behind the original Red 2 perimeter, and collection crews were already at work. It was not a job any man cared to volunteer for. Most of the corpses lay underground in bunkers or pillboxes; their swollen faces, all shades of green, yellow and blue, seemed to float like horrid balloons in the murky light. Often there was a problem determining whether a man was Japanese or American, and the burial teams would have to get down close and look at the cloth by the light of a match or a Zippo. At the collection point the Graves Registration crews took fingerprints, removed dog tags and went through pockets; the burial teams would then carry what remained over to a long row of

---

[1] Of the four Marines who won the Medal of Honor in the Tarawa campaign (Bordelon, Bonnyman, Hawkins and Shoup), only Shoup survived to have the medal placed around his neck by President Roosevelt. Before his retirement in 1963 Shoup had risen to the rank of four-star general and had served a term as Marine commandant.

shoulder-to-shoulder corpses that lay in a shallow trench. A bulldozer idled noisily nearby, its driver awaiting the signal to spread sand over the dead men's faces. Robert Sherrod watched one team drag a headless corpse up to the end of the row; there was nothing left above the shoulders but a few shreds of pale flesh. It reminded Sherrod of a slaughtered chicken, and he turned away in horror.

"What a hell of a way to die," he muttered.

"You can't pick a better way," said a Marine beside him.

Chaplain Wyeth Willard had seen many Marine cemeteries since coming out to the Pacific Theater. He remembered most vividly the one on Guadalcanal, out past Henderson Field; he had been shocked to find more than six hundred graves there. Now, as he supervised the burials on Betio, he realized there would be many more graves here than that. On the afternoon of the third day the long arm of coincidence played him a foul trick. Willard noticed a Marine curled up in death, only a few yards from the spot where he had slept the night before; he shambled over to where it lay, and began the now-routine task of preparing the body for burial. As he lifted off the helmet his eye fell on the name stenciled into the camouflaged canvas cover:

W. C. CULP

The chaplain sat down heavily on the sand and began to ponder over his part in William Culp's transfer to a line company. It was probable, he knew, that his faithful assistant would now be working alongside him—had he not thought the young man capable of greater service to his country and his Corps. And now he was burying him. Willard found it impossible to convince himself he had done the wrong thing; and yet he could not help but wish he had done nothing at all. Now he reached over and twisted the signet ring from one of the stiff fingers and unclipped a fountain pen from the breast pocket; these he would send to Culp's sister in Palm

Beach. There was nothing more he could do, except help put him under the sand.

Men wandered around looking for friends, many of whom were no longer to be found. Occasionally there were abrupt, throat-lumping reunions as filthy bestubbled men grabbed hold of one another, glad and amazed that they had made it through the 76-hour ordeal.

Souvenir hunters were already at work. Whole cases of *Asahi* beer and sake were dug out of ruined storehouses, as well as rifles and pistols, swords and flags, post cards and pornography. Someone found boxes of spanking white Imperial Navy uniforms; many of the victors immediately shed their stinking dungarees and put them on, caring little how ridiculous they looked. Sleeves hardly reached to elbows, trousers barely covered knees—but they were clean. When Julian Smith saw some of his men wandering about in this garb he promptly issued orders forbidding it, fearing that they would be shot after dark by their own sentries. Grumblingly they shed the uniforms and re-donned the sticky dungarees.

The "Tarawa Press Club" had been set up in one corner of a wrecked warehouse near the Marine command post. Using water cans for chairs and a Japanese torpedo (the same that had worried Shoup on D-day) for a desk, the correspondents were pounding out the stories that would fascinate and horrify millions of Americans for a time.

In another corner an intelligence officer, Captain Eugene Boardman, was interrogating some of the Korean prisoners. Life on Betio had been hard for them; their relationship with the Japanese was strictly master/slave. It was from these prisoners that Boardman gleaned a small bit of information that quickly became a part of the Tarawa legend: Admiral Shibasaki's grandiose boast that the Americans could not take Betio if they had a million men and a hundred years to try. Boardman also learned the answer to a question that had puzzled everyone: why the Japanese had not counterattacked on the first night, when the invaders held nothing but a couple of vulnerable toeholds on the beach. The answer was that the pre-invasion bombardment, while it failed to kill as many Japanese as the Americans expected, did ruin the island's communications system. Shibasaki had simply lacked the means to organize a general counterattack.

8

OONUKI'S
ORDEAL ENDS

Four Japanese civilian construction workers had found Oonuki hiding in the Bairiki bunker, late in the afternoon of the third day.

"*Kawa . . .*"

"*Yama,*" he had answered—*river* and *mountain* were a familiar garrison password and countersign. The civilians told him that a force of Americans (Raymond Murray's battalion) had invaded Bairiki and had moved on down the island chain. There was very little cover on Bairiki; Oonuki was afraid the five of them would be found by an enemy patrol and shot on sight. He told the four workers that it would be safer for them to wade out into the surf and wait there throughout the night. They agreed. Standing in water up to their waists, holding hands in the dark as the tide surged against them, they watched the muzzle flashes of rifles and machine guns over on Betio. It was easy to differentiate between Japanese and American weapons, because of the difference in sound, and they glumly followed the progress and failure of each of the last-ditch counterattacks. By dawn it was obvious that the remaining Japanese had been bottled up in the tail of the island.

The five of them had waded back to Bairiki at first light, their legs wrinkled from the nightlong soaking, and hid as best they could in a clump of bushes. Throughout the morning they listened to the diminishing crackle of Arisakas and the hoarse popping blasts of the American machine guns as the remnant was cut down man by man. Around noon they watched Ensign Kelly land his Hellcat on the airstrip and knew that Betio was already an American base.

By now Oonuki believed that he was actually starving to death; crushing fantasies of home and homeland began to fill his head. Unable to bear the thought that he might not see either again, he conceived the mad notion of stealing a boat from the conquerers. When he broached the idea to the civilians, two of them said they would be willing to return to Betio with him to look for food, if not the unlikely escape boat. Late that night, then, they bade farewell to the others and made their way out to the submerged sandspit. Halfway across, Oonuki stepped on a cluster of shellfish and, bending down, plucked a handful out of the water. He pried them open and greedily sucked out the meat. His two companions had not stopped, and when he looked up they were far ahead, almost swallowed up in the darkness. He dared not call out.

Oonuki reached the southeast shore of Betio just before dawn, racked with stomach cramps. Pausing now and then to vomit, he crawled inland until he found himself beside a wrecked bunker of some size. Laboriously he circled it on hands and knees, trying to find the entrance, finally collapsing from exhaustion. He fell asleep out in the open.

When he awoke, the hot sun was glaring in his face and he had the fright of his life when he looked up to see two giants grinning at him with rifles in their hands. Oonuki said later that he did not doubt he was about to die. He lay still, flat on his back, waiting for the end; but the Marines yanked him to his feet and marched him several hundred yards to the prisoner-collection point near the base of the pier. Oonuki was shocked at the enormous number of Japanese corpses he saw; and shaken, too, by the way the Marines kept staring at him, many walking right up to gawk as if he were an animal in a zoo. He did not realize that for many of them he was the first and only live Japanese they were to see up close on Betio.

Someone handed him a canteen of water and a mess kit that was brimming with warm C-rations. Only then did Tadao Oonuki begin to wonder if he might survive after all.[1]

---

[1] Oonuki was taken to Hawaii and later to a prisoner-of-war camp near Crystal City, Texas. He was returned to Japan in 1945 and is presently driving a cab in Tokyo.

9

ISLAND
OF THE MOON

The Abemama operation was a relatively bland side show. Captain James L. Jones (brother of William Jones) had landed his Recon Marines in six rubber rafts early on the morning of November 21st. It had been a miserable trip from the *Nautilus* to the beach, with rain squalls spinning the doughnut-shaped rafts around like chips in a whirlpool. Only after four hours of the most strenuous effort did the Marines get themselves ashore—at the very last point before they would have been fouled in a barrier reef.

Jones was not sure there were any Japanese on the island; his twofold mission was to find out and, if the answer was yes, to stake out a suitable beach for a battalion landing after Betio fell. At daybreak the presence of the enemy was confirmed when Jones found an Imperial Navy whaleboat in a cove. He had his men punch holes in it with their bayonets, ruining it as a getaway craft.

Accompanying the Marines was an Australian Army lieutenant named George Hard, who had lived in the Gilberts and knew the people of Abemama. Creeping along now with the Marines, he spotted a couple of natives casually loping along the trail, heading their way. Hard and the Marines waited in the bushes out of sight—for they had no notion how the Abemamese had reacted to the Greater East Asia Co-prosperity Sphere. When the two men were almost on them, Hard stood up and greeted them in their own language.

"Why, my *word*—isn't it Mr. Hard?" one of them is reported to have said in unruffled missionary-taught English. "But were you wise to visit us just now, Mr. Hard?"

From this jaunty fellow the Australian learned that there were twenty-five Japanese on the next islet (part of Abemama) and that they were well entrenched around a radio station. That night the Marines spotted winking lights a few hundred yards out to sea. Jones figured it was probably a Japanese submarine, come to evacuate the garrison. But with their whaleboat ruined, the garrison was trapped.

The following morning Jones and his men, guided by the two natives, moved on the encampment two miles away, as *Nautilus* stood offshore, ready to provide supporting fire with her deck gun. The camp was separated from the adjoining islet by a shallow channel; as the Marines started across, their column was suddenly raked by long-range automatic fire. Jones signaled Commander Irvin for support and the *Nautilus* gun crew responded with seventy rounds, enabling the Marines to make the crossing without a casualty. When they approached the camp itself, however, a burst of fire wounded two men and Jones called a halt. General Smith had given him specific orders to avoid an engagement; he decided now that the thing to do was to sit tight until the 26th, when the battalion landing was tentatively scheduled.

Captain Jones did not have to sit for long. On the morning of the 24th a young native showed up to announce dramatically that all the Japanese were dead. He asked for a cigarette; it was given him, and he began to tell Jones a strange story indeed. The day before, he said, he had hidden near the radio station and watched while the garrison commander, a captain, assembled his troops in two ranks and began to deliver a speech. The native reported that the officer had held a sword in one hand, a pistol in the other, and that in his violent gesturing the pistol went off and the bullet killed him. Completely demoralized now, the sailors began literally digging their own graves; when they were done, they lay down in them and shot themselves.

Captain Jones led his men to the camp and found that it was so. Not a man remained alive. The Marines finished the burial job, and the people of Abemama began to creep warily out of hiding. Before an hour had passed, eager brown youngsters were shinnying up the trees to throw down coconuts for the Marines. Later, young girls with round bare breasts stood together in their sailcloth skirts and serenaded them with hymns the British missionaries had taught them.

General Julian C. Smith, having had no word from Jones, decided to go ahead with the landing on the tiny atoll. He sent McLeod's 3/6, the battalion that had been the least bruised on Betio. Before anyone could get ashore, however, Captain Jones came rafting across the waters with the happy news that the garrison was dead to a man and the atoll was in Marine hands.

In the soft afternoon sunshine McLeod and his men had to wade a few hundred yards across a reef, a situation that reminded everyone of Betio on the first day and the second morning. There the similarity ended, as the Marines sloshed ashore to be handed opened coconuts by bare-breasted maidens. The island was clean, the air sweet. Everything was quite unlike the hideous place they had left behind that morning.

10

THE GENERALS INSPECT

A wondrous sight now greeted the eyes of the Marines on Betio: the transports were sailing into the lagoon.

Orders went out to all battalion commanders: *Prepare to board ship.* As the troops trudged along the pier, ready to board Higgins boats for the trip out to the ships, many of the men stared in red-rimmed astonishment at the water on either side. The reef—as we have already seen—had simply disappeared; the ordinary seasonal tide had washed in, the very tide they had needed so desperately on the first two days. Sea water was slapping up against the coconut-log wall, and there was no beach at all.

Holland Smith arrived by plane later in the day. On his way over to the command post, as he wrote later, he "passed boys who had lived yesterday a thousand times and looked older than their fathers. Dirty, unshaven, with gaunt, almost sightless eyes, they had survived the ordeal but it had chilled their souls."

Julian Smith joined him for the flag raising. Two topless palm trees had been picked for the double ceremony, and rope pulleys rigged. Major F. L. G. Holland, the Britisher whose warning about the tide had been overruled, happened to have a Union Jack in his possession for just this moment.

There was one unscheduled delay, as Pfc. James Williams (Birmingham, Ala.) stepped forward and raised his bugle, ready to sound Colors.

"Hold it," said Julian Smith. Williams was wearing a set of Imperial Navy togs; he had not got the word. "Take those damn things off."

Everyone waited as Williams persuaded a bystander to strip on the spot and hand over his filthy dungarees for the ceremony. When this had been attended to, Sergeant Vito Million (Philadelphia) and Corporal Mickey Frankenstein (Los Angeles) took hold of the ropes and slowly raised the Stars and Stripes to the top of the truncated, shrapnel-pocked tree; the Union Jack followed a moment or two later. A brisk trade wind snapped both flags straight out. As Pfc. Williams' thin clear notes sounded hauntingly across the blasted desolation of the island, men turned from their work to stand at attention. Some of the wounded beside Brukardt's hospital struggled to their feet; the rest, those who could, turned their heads or merely discarded cigarettes and lay stiffly as a sign of respect for the flag they had fought and suffered for. The riflemen waiting atop the pier heard the notes too, and some of the weariness went out of them; everyone knew what it had cost to plant those bits of cloth.

The two generals began to tour the battlefield now, accompanied by a few correspondents, including Sherrod. Holland Smith wanted to take a close look at some of the pillboxes overlooking the beach.

"The Germans never built anything this good in France," he remarked after inspecting a few. "No wonder the Japs were sitting back here laughing at us. They never dreamed we could take this place."

Later they came across two clusters of dead Marines, collected for burial. Holland Smith counted them; there were twenty-three in one pile, twenty-eight in the other. Someone had scratched a few letters on a board and set it up over them:

I & K Companies, 3rd Bn, 2nd Div

A little farther down the beach they came across an amtrac bearing the name "Worried Mind." Inside lay six dead Marines, with three more on the sand beside it. Holland Smith shook his head in dismay.

"What do you suppose the totals are going to be, Julian?"

"Somewhere around a thousand, I imagine. Wounded will come to more than twice that."

Holland Smith stood still for a moment, gazing across the dead at still another string of bunkers and pillboxes. "How did they do it, Julian—how did those boys ever take this place?"

He turned to go and, almost directly in his path, a kind of answer met his gaze. A lone Marine lay there, with one arm flung across the top of the sea wall; inches away from his outstretched fingers stood a blue flag—a beach marker, signaling the boatwaves where to land. The Marine had planted it with his life. Holland Smith trudged on past the body, tears running down his cheeks.

"You can't help but win," he said, "when you've got men like that on your side."

The inspecting party followed along, leaving the eloquent tableau behind, and Robert Sherrod paused long enough to scribble in his notebook: *How much every man in battle owes to every other man! How easy to see on the battlefield that we are in this thing together!*

11

LOST AT SEA

The day after Betio was secured a disaster struck the fleet at sea. In the space of twenty-three minutes more American sailors were lost than Marines were killed in the first two days of the battle for Betio.

The time was 4:35 a.m., November 24th. There was a gentle swell and a light southeasterly breeze. Clouds obscured the moon. The escort carrier *Liscome Bay*, commanded by Captain Irving D. Wiltsie, was steaming along twenty miles southwest of Makin when one of its screen destroyers reported a flashing light on the western horizon. The destroyer was sent to investigate. Shortly afterward the battleship *New Mexico* reported a radar contact to the north, which faded after four minutes. There was either a whale nearby or a submarine; and if it was a sub, it was definitely not an American sub.

At 5:05 *Liscome Bay* went to general quarters, a routine move at morning twilight in dangerous waters. The pilots were already assembled at flight quarters, since it had been planned to launch search groups at sunrise. At 5:08 the destroyer reported that the flashing light was probably a beacon-light or a float. It was believed to have been dropped by an enemy plane to signal a submarine that American ships were in the vicinity. At 5:10 *Liscome Bay* turned right to course 055° for flight operations—heading northeast now—and made

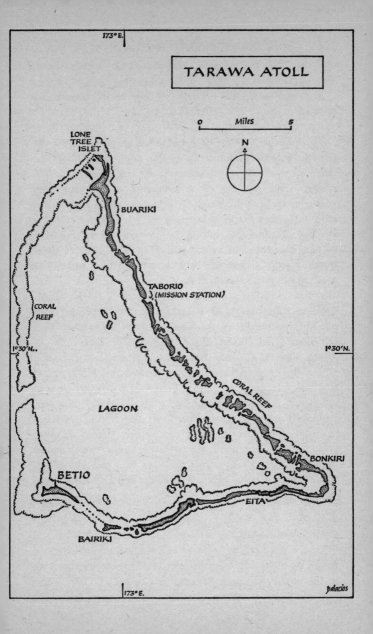

of herself a perfect target for Lieutenant Commander Sunao Tabata, commanding officer of the submarine *I-175*.

At 5:13, as dawn was beginning to light up the horizon, one of the *Liscome Bay* lookouts cried:

"Torpedo! Torpedo!"

There was no time for Captain Wiltsie to maneuver the carrier; the torpedo hit amidships on the port side, setting off a string of horrendous explosions in the magazine and fuel-storage areas, sending up a column of orange flame that witnesses said rose hundreds of feet in the air. A few seconds later the ship's bomb stowage went up and *Liscome Bay* burst apart with a roar, hurling men, planes and molten debris so high that the deck of the battleship *New Mexico*, fifteen hundred yards to leeward, was showered with fragments of steel, clothing and human flesh.

Witnesses on the other ships assumed that everybody aboard the carrier must surely have died in the ferocious series of explosions; but many survived, and were only too ready to obey the order of Lieutenant Commander Bodler, the senior surviving officer, to abandon ship. The surrounding water, covered with a film of gasoline and oil, was ignited by a blazing plane that fell overboard as the ship canted to starboard; many of the men in the water were burned to death, while others were injured by underwater explosions as the ship started to settle.

Twenty-three minutes after the torpedo struck, the shattered hulk sank sternfirst, hissing slowly into a two-thousand-fathom grave with 19 planes and 644 men still aboard, including Rear Admiral Henry A. Mullinix and Captain Wiltsie.[1]

---

[1] *I-175* got away but was sunk three months later during the Marshalls campaign.

12

THE WRAP-UP

As the sun dipped toward the horizon on the 24th, most of the troop-laden transports had already passed through the narrow channel of the lagoon into the open sea, their bows pointing toward Hawaii.

Other troops still had work to do; Betio had been conquered but the battle of Tarawa Atoll was not quite finished. Raymond Murray's 2nd Battalion, Sixth Marines, had been chasing the enemy remnant up the atoll chain for several days now, wading across sand bars and reefs that connected the small islands. At Taborio, three-quarters of the way up the chain, the battalion was met by a friendly and curious crowd of Tarawans who, along wih a couple of French missionaries, confirmed the passage of a sizable Japanese force.

About two hundred of the natives attached themselves to Murray's column, obviously looking on the expedition as a huge lark, and eagerly anticipating the battle that would occur when the Marines cornered their prey. Colonel Murray put them to work as bearers; one fellow named Tutu did the interpreting and kept order among the natives (he had learned English studying at a medical college on Fiji). When the battalion and its brown-skinned bearers stopped for the night, the two groups—discreetly separate, for there were some fifty women present—serenaded each other with songs.

It was not until late afternoon of the 26th that the column reached the next-to-last island of the atoll, Buariki. As two of the infantry companies took up defensive positions for the night, the third company went forward into thick brush to look for the enemy. At dusk they ran into a Japanese patrol, and in the brief fire fight two Marines were wounded and several enemy sailors were seen to fall; but with darkness rapidly closing in, the action was broken off.

Murray attacked with two companies the next morning. His biggest problem turned out to be the Tarawans. The dusky, bushy-haired men all seemed intent on demonstrating their courage and kept getting in the way. Fortunately the women were content to remain behind in a deserted village, where the first-aid station had been set up. They made palm-frond pillows for the wounded, fanned away flies, brought fresh water and generally helped out, while Tutu proved to the Navy corpsmen that he knew how to handle surgical instruments. The fighting did not last long; the Japanese sailors were killed one by one in their taro-pit positions.

One small patch of territory remained to be conquered before Operation *Galvanic* came to a close. This was Lone Tree Islet, which resembled an island in a shipwreck cartoon. The Marines could plainly see eight enemy sailors sitting listlessly around the lone tree itself, waiting for the end. Murray sent a squad across the narrow channel, and the last of the die-hards were exterminated, almost casually.[1]

* * *

Thus, in less than a week, the Americans had obtained three firm footholds in the Central Pacific—Tarawa, Makin and Abemama—and would soon make use of these bases as jumpoff points for further conquests, in the long and bloody drive toward the enemy's heartland. The lessons learned at Betio had been learned the hard way: the need for more

---

[1] Japanese (and Korean) casualties on Tarawa: 4,690 killed, 146 captured—only 17 of them Japanese. Marine (and U. S. Navy corpsmen) casualties on Tarawa: 1,027 killed, 2,292 wounded, 88 missing and presumed dead.

accurate and powerful bombardment, more amtracs, better radios, more flame throwers and demolitions, better tank-infantry co-ordination, better boat traffic control—and, most important of all, more thorough planning. The knowledge and experience gained in the amphibious-warfare laboratory of Betio led to changes that were to reduce substantially the cost of the many Pacific landings that followed.

The question can fairly be asked: might not those lessons have been learned in the Marshalls? The answer is yes; but the notion of going straight into that redoubt, by-passing the Gilberts, had seemed to the American high command at that moment in the war far too risky a venture. (As Marine Corps historian Henry I. Shaw, Jr., put it, "In the light of what happened later in the Pacific fighting—and not too much later—it is hard for the armchair strategist to see why Tarawa was a necessary target, but no amount of hindsight can match the pressures and realities of the existing situation.")

The last of the Marine battalions was coming aboard. It took some of the men a long time to pull themselves up the cargo nets, dog-tired and weak as they were; sailors leaned over the rail, ready to haul each Marine over onto the deck. By 5 p.m. the convoy was at sea, Hawaii-bound. The sun, just dipping below the horizon, sent quivering fans of light across the water. On the weather decks of the troopships, the squawkboxes droned routinely, "Now hear this. Sweepers, man your brooms. Clean sweep-down fore and aft. . . ."

The veterans stood at the rails, gazing bleary-eyed into the distance. Tarawa Atoll, a hazy dream of the horizon, sank slowly out of sight.

AFTERWORD

The two-thousand-mile voyage to Hawaii was an odd post-script to the horror of the battle itself. Every day there were funerals aboard the transports, with flag-draped bodies slipping into rushing waters. The transports reeked of the rotting-corpse stench that clung to the survivors' clothing; no new dungarees had been issued and almost everyone had lost his pack in the shuffle.

At Pearl Harbor the wounded were unloaded and transferred to the naval hospital in Honolulu. The rest of the convoy sailed on two hundred miles farther, to the easternmost of the Hawaiian Islands, arriving on December 5th. They were taken by truck convoy to the site of their new camp, called Camp Tarawa, located in the lofty saddle between the dormant volcanoes Mauna Kea and Mauna Loa. The site was, surprisingly, cold and barren—nothing like the paradise they had half expected.

For the next three weeks, starting from scratch, the men of the 2nd Marine Division worked steadily in chill rain and mist, sleeping without blankets, building a camp for themselves. Julian Smith tried to borrow blankets from the U. S. Army warehouse in Hilo, but had to appeal to Lieutenant General Richardson at Makalapa before he got them. The Marines were understandably bitter about the seeming inappropriateness of the site, sixty-five miles away from the nearest city (not to mention the business of the blankets); but there was a reason for putting the camp where it was. First of all, the cool climate was beneficial to the many men still in the grip of Guadalcanal malaria. Second, the vast Parker cattle-ranch ranges surrounding the camp offered perfect training terrain for the next battle, which Smith had already learned was to take place on mountainous Saipan. Finally, the camp's isolation gave the Marines time to make an important adjustment. They had to come to understand, many of them, that Hawaiian residents of Japanese ancestry were not to be equated with the kind of people they had slaughtered by the thousands on Guadalcanal, Tulagi and Tarawa. No one spoke of this officially, and it seems farfetched today; but it was considered a serious matter at the time.

The details of the battle for Tarawa came as a shock to the American public, stirring waves of awe and anger. Three thousand men dead or wounded in three days of fighting, to capture an island nobody had even heard of—it seemed hardly worth the price. Angry editorials appeared in newspapers from coast to coast with the phrases "Bloody Betio" and "Terrible Tarawa," and there was talk about "the Tarawa fiasco." There was also the threat of a congressional investigation, as the public struggled to absorb the stunning casualty lists. (At Pearl Harbor a naval board of inquiry asked Kelly Turner to justify his decisions regarding the D-day tide factor, and Turner could only admit, finally, that he had taken a calculated risk and lost.) In due time the commandant of the Marine Corps came forward with a public statement:

"No one regrets the losses more than the Marine Corps itself," said Lieutenant General A. A. Vandegrift. "No one realizes more than does the Marine Corps that there is no Royal Road to Tokyo. We must steel our people to the same realization."

Tarawa was forgotten soon enough, of course, as the newspapers printed the details of other campaigns with even longer casualty lists. But those men who had survived the battle for Betio Island would always doubt that any of the later battles could match theirs for sheer concentrated destruction.

Following the war, the controversy flared briefly with the publication of Holland Smith's *Coral and Brass,* in which the retired general claimed that "Tarawa should have been bypassed. Its capture was a terrible waste of life and effort. Rabaul, in the South Pacific, and Truk, in the Central Pacific, both far stronger and more vital bases, were bypassed without any danger to our rear." It should be noted, however, that General Smith's criticism was developed in hindsight; he never raised the slightest objection during the planning stages of the campaign. And he was virtually alone in his attitude; every historian, journalist and student who has ever researched the campaigns in the Central Pacific agrees that there had to be a Tarawa. Henry I. Shaw, Jr., sums it up about as well as anyone:

"It was no fluke that the operations in the Marshalls ten weeks after *Galvanic* were conducted with fewer casualties and in less time against similar targets. In a very real sense, the men who died taking Betio Island had saved the lives of countless other Americans. The senior officers who led *Galvanic* drove their staffs hard from the moment the fighting ended in the Gilberts to find, dissect, and remedy every fault, in every category, that had been exposed. Seldom have men been so honestly self-critical and so dedicated to finding error and providing solutions. . . .

"If there had been no assault on Tarawa, there would have been another fortress island where the painful lessons it taught would have been learned. The success of every subsequent operation in the Pacific owed a debt to the men who had died to take the tiny atoll and to the men who survived the battle to fight again."

In the early 1960s an American writer named James Ramsey Ullman traveled the South Seas to gather material for a book, and one of the places he visited was Tarawa. The Gilberts are quite isolated from the major trading areas of the Pacific, far from any air or shipping lanes, and Ullman had to wait in the Marshalls for several weeks before he was able to charter a small ship to carry him the two-hundred-odd miles to Tarawa.

After many days at sea, the lookout finally shouted the Central Pacific equivalent of *Land ho* as up over the horizon came the northernmost of the Gilberts, Makin Atoll. For hours it seemed to drift past, then finally disappeared. From this point on the radioman tried repeatedly to contact Radio Tarawa but could raise only static. At sunset a crisp British-accented voice crackled startlingly through the deckhouse of the small ship. "We can see you," said Radio Tarawa.

The fringe of reef came up fast, and so did darkness, as it always does in those climes. At the end of the tree-lined jetty, a white obelisk loomed in the dusk; this, the first Betio landmark that is visible from sea, is a memorial to the men of the 2nd Marine Division who died in the long-ago battle. As the ship made its passage through the outer reef into the lagoon in the last glimmer of daylight, the order came from shore to spend the night at anchor; Her Majesty's Customs would be out in the morning. Tarawa's fleet of outrigger canoes kept more flexible hours, however; no sooner had the ship entered the lagoon than a procession was following along, aglow with lanterns and torches. When the ship dropped anchor they closed in softly, forming a great twinkling fan about the ship, and the natives began passing out welcoming gifts of breadfruit and papaya.

Ullman lounged around the island for two days, sitting in the shade of the coconut palms, wading in the silken water. He was not particularly interested in Betio as a battle site, although he did think about it from time to time. "It is a familiar irony," he wrote, "that old battlefields are often the quietest and gentlest of places. It is true of Gettysburg. It is true of Cannae, Chalons, Austerlitz, Verdun. And it is true of Tarawa."

Although the bodies of the bulldozer-buried Marines have long since been disinterred and taken back to the States, natives digging beside William D. Hawkins Field occasionally uncover skeletons with dog tags on them. Whenever this happens, the British authorities dutifully notify the Pentagon. Aside from these rare finds the only visible signs of the battle are Shibasaki's two-story command post, its side still black from the scorchings of the flame throwers, and the rusted frame of an amtrac that emerges ghostlike at low tide.

BIBLIOGRAPHY

Battle for Tarawa, by Seth Bailey (Monarch).

The Battle for Tarawa, by James Stockman (Marine Corps monograph).

Battle Report: The End of an Empire, by Walter Karig (Rinehart).

Battles Lost and Won, by Hanson Baldwin (Harper & Row).

Betio Beachhead, by Earl J. Wilson et al. (Putnam).

Big Yankee, by Michael Blankfort (Little, Brown).

Central Pacific Drive, by Shaw, Nalty, Turnbladh (Marine Corps).

Coral and Brass, by Holland M. Smith and Percy Finch (Scribner).

The Epic of Tarawa, by W. Richardson (Odhams Press).

Follow Me! The Story of the 2nd Marine Division, by Richard A. Johnston (Random House).

The Fortunes of War, by Andrew Rooney (Little, Brown).

History of U. S. Naval Operations in World War II, Vol. 7, by Samuel Eliot Morison (Little, Brown).

How They Won the War in the Pacific, by Edwin P. Hoyt (Weybright & Talley).

The Island War, by Frank Hough (Lippincott).

Japan's Imperial Conspiracy, by David Bergamini (Morrow).

The Leathernecks Come Through, by W. Wyeth Willard (Revell).

The Marines' War, by Fletcher Pratt (Sloan).

Seizure of the Gilberts and Marshalls, by Crowl and Love (Department of the Army).

Strong Men Armed, by Robert Leckie (Random House).

Tarawa: A Legend Is Born, by Henry I. Shaw, Jr. (Ballantine).

Tarawa: The Story of a Battle, by Robert Sherrod (Duell, Sloan and Pearce).

Tarawa: The Toughest Battle in Marine Corps History, by Dick Hannah (U. S. Camera).

The United States Marine Corps in World War II, by S. E. Smith (Random House).

The U. S. Marines and Amphibious War, by Isely and Crowl (Princeton University Press).

The War with Japan, by Charles Bateson (Ure Smith).

Where the Bong Tree Grows, by James Ramsey Ullman (World).

Interviews and correspondence with survivors.

Marine Corps historical files.

INDEX